THE WONDER OF WHIFFLING

THE WONDER OF WHIFFLING

And other extraordinary words in the English language

ADAM JACOT DE BOINOD

Illustrations by Sandra Howgate

PARTICULAR BOOKS

PARTICULAR BOOKS

Published by the Penguin Group
Penguin Books Ltd, 80 Strand, London WC2R 0RL, England
Penguin Group (USA) Inc., 375 Hudson Street, New York, New York 10014, USA
Penguin Group (Canada), 90 Eglinton Avenue East, Suite 700, Toronto, Ontario, Canada M4P 2Y3 (a division of Pearson Penguin Canada Inc.)
Penguin Ireland, 25 St Stephen's Green, Dublin 2, Ireland (a division of Penguin Books Ltd)
Penguin Group (Australia), 250 Camberwell Road, Camberwell, Victoria 3124, Australia (a division of Pearson Australia Group Pty Ltd)
Penguin Books India Pvt Ltd, 11 Community Centre, Panchsheel Park, New Delhi – 110 017, India
Penguin Group (NZ), 67 Apollo Drive, Rosedale, North Shore 0632, New Zealand (a division of Pearson New Zealand Ltd)
Penguin Books (South Africa) (Pty) Ltd, 24 Sturdee Avenue, Rosebank, Johannesburg 2196, South Africa

Penguin Books Ltd, Registered Offices: 80 Strand, London WC2R 0RL, England

www.penguin.com

First published 2009
1

Set in 9.2/13 pt Adobe Caslon Pro,
with Monotype Festival Titling and Monotype Grotesque light condensed
Typeset by Andrew Barker Information Design
Printed in England by Clays Ltd, St Ives plc

ISBN: 978-0-140-51585-5

CONTENTS

FOREWORD

While I was working on my last two books, scouring libraries and second hand bookshops, riffling through reference books from around the world to find words with unusual and delightful meanings, I kept coming across splendid English dictionaries too. Not just the mighty twenty-volume *Oxford English Dictionary*, but all kinds of collections covering dialect, jargon, slang and subsidiary areas, such as Jamaican or Newfoundland English.

My passion for the arcane was renewed as I confronted the remarkable wealth of words in our language, from its origins in Anglo-Saxon, through Old and Middle English and Tudor–Stuart, then on to the rural dialects collected so lovingly by Victorian lexicographers, the argot of nineteenth-century criminals, slang from the two world wars, right up to contemporary life and the jargon that has grown up around such diverse activities as darts, birding and working in an office. When I was offered the chance, it seemed only right to gather the best examples together and complete my trilogy: bringing, as it were, the original idea home.

Some of our English words mean much the same as they always have. Others have changed beyond recognition, such as **racket**, which originally meant the palm of the hand; **grape**, a hook for gathering fruit; or **muddle**, to wallow in mud. Then there are those words that have fallen out of use, but would undoubtedly make handy additions to any vocabulary today. Don't most of us know a **blatteroon**, a person who will not stop talking, not to mention a **shot-clog**, a drinking companion only tolerated because he pays for the drinks? And if one day we feel **mumpish**, sullenly angry, shouldn't we seek the company of a **grinagog**, one who is always grinning?

The dialects of Britain provide a wealth of coinages. In the Midlands, for example, we find a **jaisy**, a polite and effeminate man, and in Yorkshire a **stridewallops**, a tall and awkward woman. If you tuck too much into the clotted cream in Cornwall you might end up **ploffy**, plump; in Shropshire, hold back on the beer or you might develop **joblocks**, fleshy, hanging cheeks; and down in Wiltshire hands that have been left too long in the washtub are **quobbled**. The Geordies have the evocative word **dottle** for the tobacco left in the pipe after smoking, and in Lincolnshire **charmings** are paper and rag chewed into small pieces by mice. In Suffolk to **nuddle** is to walk alone with the head held low; and in Hampshire to **vuddle** is to spoil a child by injudicious petting. And don't we all know someone who is **crambazzled** (Yorkshire), prematurely aged through drink and a dissolute life?

Like English itself, my research hasn't stopped at the shores of the Channel. Our language is arguably the most widespread of all, and second only to Mandarin in terms of usage. Varieties of our basic tongue thrive all over the globe and certain locales have come up with charming and serviceable words that could usefully be imported back. How about a **call-dog** (Jamaican English), a fish too small for human consumption or a **twack** (Newfoundland English) a shopper who looks at goods, inquires about prices, but buys nothing.

Slang from elsewhere offers us everything from a **waterboy** (US police), a boxer who can be bribed or coerced into losing, to a **shubie** (Australian), someone who buys surfing gear and clothing but doesn't actually surf. In Canada, a **cougar** describes an older woman on the prowl for a younger man, while in the US a **quirkyalone** is someone who doesn't fall in love easily, but waits for the right person to come along.

The language of specialist activities, from sport to card games, could have filled another volume. I've contented myself instead with a pick of my favourites, from **fliffis**, the gymnast's term for a twisting double somersault to **squopped**, the term for a free tiddlywink that lands on another wink. The stage has a splendid private jargon, from **pong**, to speak in blank verse after forgetting one's lines, to **gravy**, easy laughs from a friendly audience. Perhaps only the criminal fraternity has more, with everything from the **vamper**, a thief who deliberately starts fights between others in order to rob people in the confusion, to the **pappy**, the elderly man with baggy clothes and saggy pockets who is a pickpocket's ideal victim.

Returning to the mainstream it's been interesting to note those words coined by major literary figures such as **kankedort** (Chaucer), an awkward situation; **fleshment** (Shakespeare), excitement from a first success; **ferrule** (Dickens), the metal tip on an umbrella; **oubliette** (Scott), a dungeon whose only entrance is in the ceiling and **mud-honey** (Tennyson) the dirty pleasures of men about town.

Along the way I've discovered some intriguing people: from the **parnel**, a priest's mistress, through the **applesquire**, the male servant of a prostitute, to the **screever**, a writer of begging letters. If the first two of these are now largely historical, the third certainly isn't, nor is the **slapsauce**, the person who enjoys eating fine food or the **chafferer**, the salesman who enjoys talking while making a sale.

As for **whiffling**, well, that turned out to be a word with a host of meanings. In eighteenth-century Oxford and Cambridge, a whiffler was one who examined candidates for degrees, while elsewhere a whiffler was an officer who cleared the way for a procession, as well as being the name for the man with the whip in Morris dancing. The word also means trifling or pettifogging, to blow or scatter with gusts of air, to move or think erratically, as well as applying to geese descending rapidly from a height once the decision to land has been made. In the seventeenth century a whiffler was a smoker of tobacco; in the underworld slang of Victorian times, one who cried out in pain; while in the cosier world of P. G. Wodehouse, whiffled was what you were when you'd had one too many of Jeeves's special cocktails.

So let's raise a **brendice**, a cup in which a person's health is drunk, to this extraordinary language of ours, crammed full of words most **ostrobogulous** (bizarre and interesting), the study of which could keep us occupied from **beetle-belch** to **cockshut**. As a self-confessed **bower-bird** (one who collects an astonishing array of sometimes useless objects), I've had great fun putting together this collection. I sincerely hope that you enjoy reading it, and that it saves you both from **mulligrubs**, depression of spirits and, of course, **onomatomania**, vexation in having difficulty finding the right word.

Adam Jacot de Boinod

AUTHOR'S NOTE

In compiling this book I've been keen to distinguish formalized English from the informal and have pinpointed from where a word originates and when it came into the English language (with dates in brackets to mark its first printed reference in English, and with the letter b. stating that the word came into our language before a specific time). Source languages are also included here when a word has been loaned. An English county indicates dialect, which may well have spread into other areas. As before, I've done my level best to check the accuracy of all the words included, but for any comments or even favourite examples of words of your own please contact me direct at the book's website, **www.thewonderofwhiffling.com**. (There were some helpful responses to my previous books, for which I remain very grateful.)

ACKNOWLEDGEMENTS

I am deeply grateful to the following people for their advice and help: Giles Andreae, Kate Lawson and Sarah McDougall. In particular I must thank my illustrator Sandra Howgate, my agent, Peter Straus, my excellent editorial team at Penguin – my editor Georgina Laycock and Ruth Stimson and Helen Conford, and once again my collaborator Mark McCrum for his invaluable work on the text.

CLATTERFARTS AND JAISIES

Getting acquainted

Great talkers should be crop'd,
for they have no need of ears

(Franklin: *Poor Richard's Almanack* 1738)

Once upon a time, your first contact with someone was likely to be face to face. These days you're as likely to get together via the computer:

floodgaters people who send you email inquiries and, after receiving any kind of response, begin swamping you with multiple messages of little or no interest

digerati those who have, or claim to have, expertise in computers or the Internet

disemvowel to remove the vowels from a word in an email, text message, etc, to abbreviate it

bitslag all the useless rubble one must plough through on the Net to get to the rich information ore

ham legitimate email messages (as opposed to spam)

DOG AND BONE

Possibly the most used English word of greeting – **hello** – only came into common usage with the arrival of the telephone. Its inventor, Alexander Graham Bell, felt that the usual Victorian greeting of **'How do you do?'** was too long and old-fashioned for his new device. He suggested the sailor's cry **ahoy!** as the best way to answer his machine and operators at the first exchange did just that. But ahoy! didn't prove popular because it felt too abrupt. Compromise was soon reached with **hello!**, a word that came straight from the hunting-field. But could Bell ever have foreseen some of the ways in which his device would come to be used?

Hollywood no (US slang 1992) a lack of response (to a proposal, phone call, message etc.)

scotchie (South African slang) a 'missed call' which communicates some pre-arranged message or requires the receiver to call back at their expense, thereby saving the first caller the cost of the call

fox hole (UK slang 2007) the area beneath one's desk (in these days of open-plan offices) where telephone calls can take place peacefully

SNAIL MAIL

Of course, the old-fashioned letter still has its uses, as these Service slang words indicate: the key one being, in these days of retentive hard drives, that once you've destroyed your message, it leaves no trace:

yam yum a love letter
giz to read a pal's letter to his girlfriend; to offer advice
gander a look through the mail, a glance over another's shoulder at a letter or paper
flimsies the rice paper on which important messages are written and which can be eaten without discomfort in case of capture

VISITING HOURS

Or you can do that wonderfully traditional thing and pay a call in person:

pasteboard (1864) to leave one's visiting card at someone's residence
cohonestation (17C) honouring with one's company
gin pennant (Royal Navy slang) a green and white triangular pennant flown to indicate an invitation on board for drinks

GR8

The arrival of mobile phones on the scene led immediately to some interesting usages. In the first wave of texting came shortened versions of much-used phrases:

F2T	free to talk
AFAIK	as far as I know
T+	think positive
BCNU	be seeing you
HAND	have a nice day
KIT	keep in touch
CUL8R	see you later
ZZZ	tired, bored

When people switched to predictive text, they discovered the phenomenon of the phone's software coming up with the wrong word; most famously **book** for **cool** (so teenagers started describing their hipper friends as 'book'). Other **textonyms** include:

lips for **kiss**
shag for **rich**
carnage for **barmaid**
poisoned for **Smirnoff**

A LITTLE SOMETHING

A gift, however small, will always go down well:

toecover (1948) an inexpensive and useless present
xenium (Latin 1706) a gift given to a guest
exennium (Old English law) a gift given at New Year
groundbait (Royal Navy slang) a box of chocolates or something similar given to a lady friend in pursuit of a greater prize

DIGNITY AND PRIDE

In the US, the knuckles touched together are called, variously, **closed-fist high fives, knuckle buckles** or **fist jabs**. Done horizontally, the gesture is called a **pound**; vertically it's the **dap** (which some say is an acronym of 'dignity and pride'). Other greetings, of course, involve words, but hopefully not misunderstandings:

dymsassenach (Cheshire) a mangled Welsh phrase meaning 'I don't understand English'
shaggledick (Australian slang) an affectionate greeting for someone who is familiar but whose name doesn't come to mind
take me with you (Tudor–Stuart) let me understand you clearly
thuten (Middle English 1100–1500) to say 'thou' to a person, to become a close friend

ALL RIGHT, MATE?

You never get a second chance to make a first impression, so be aware of how you're coming across:

corduroy voice (US 1950s) a voice that continually fluctuates between high and low (from the up-and-down ridges in corduroy)
yomp (Cheshire) to shout with the mouth wide open
snoach (1387) to speak through the nose
psellism (1799) an indistinct pronunciation, such as produced by a lisp or by stammering

RABBIT, RABBIT

Though there are always those who just can't help themselves:

macrology (1586) much talk with little to say
clatterfart (1552) a babbler, chatterer
chelp (Northern and Midlands 19C) to chatter or speak out of turn
blatteroon (1645) a person who will not stop talking
clitherer (Galway) a woman with too much to say
air one's vocabulary (*c.*1820) to talk for the sake of talking

SMOOTH CUSTOMER

Chit-chat apart, good manners always go down well (however bogus they may be):

garbist (1640) one who is adept at engaging in polite behaviour
jaisy (Midlands) a polite, effeminate man
sahlifahly (Nottinghamshire) to make flattering speeches
court holy water (1519) to say fair words without sincere intention; to flatter
deipnosophist (1656) a skilful dinner conversationalist

PETER PIPER: TONGUE TWISTERS

There are tongue twisters in every language. These phrases are designed to be difficult to say and to get harder and harder as you say them faster. They're not just for fun. Therapists and elocution teachers use them to tame speech impediments and iron out strong accents.

Repeat after me (being particularly careful with the last one) . . .

Sister Sue sells sea shells. She sells sea shells on shore. The shells she sells. Are sea shells she sees. Sure she sees shells she sells

You've known me to light a night light on a light night like tonight. There's no need to light a night light on a light night like tonight, for a night light's a slight light on tonight's light night

I'm not the pheasant plucker. I'm the pheasant plucker's son. I'm only plucking pheasants till the pheasant plucker comes

Some short words or phrases 'become' tongue-twisters when repeated, a number of times fast:

Thin Thing
French Friend
Red Leather, Yellow Leather
Unique New York
Sometimes Sunshine
Irish Wristwatch
Big Whip

CLEVER CLOGS

But let's not go too far. Nothing, surely is worse than those people who put on airs and graces ...

nosism (1829) the use of the royal 'we' in speaking of oneself
peel eggs (*c.*1860) to stand on ceremony
gedge (Scotland 1733) to talk idly with stupid gravity
godwottery (1939) the affected use of archaic language

... or claim to know more than they do:

ultracrepidarian (1819) one who makes pronouncements on topics beyond his knowledge
raw-gabbit (Scotland 1911) speaking confidently on a subject of which one is ignorant
to talk like the back of a cigarette card (UK slang 1930s) to pretend to greater knowledge than one has (the cards carried a picture on the front and a description or potted biography on the back)

MANNER OF SPEAKING

All's fair in love and war, but a good classical education provides a conversational armoury that is hard to match:

diasyrm (1678) a rhetorical device of damning with faint praise
sermocination (1753) a speaker who quickly answers his own question
paraleipsis (Ancient Greek 1586) mentioning something by saying you won't mention it
eutrapely (1596) pleasantness in conversation (one of the seven virtues enumerated by Aristotle)

IRONY IN THE SOUL

Other tricks can leave the Average Joe standing . . .

charientism (1589) an insult so gracefully veiled as to seem unintended
asteism (1589) polite and ingenuous mockery
to talk packthread (b.1811) to use indecent language well hidden, as a tinker carefully folds and tucks thread back away into his pack of goods
vilipend (1529) verbally to belittle someone

. . . and make the rest of us look like idiots:

onomatomania (1895) vexation in having difficulty in finding the right word
palilalia (1908) a speech disorder characterized by the repetition of words, phrases or sentences
verbigeration (1886) the repetition of the same word or phrase in a meaningless fashion (as a symptom of mental disease)

WORD JOURNEYS

Originally these common words and phrases meant something very different:

constipate (16C from Latin) to crowd together into a narrow room
anthology (17C from Ancient Greek) a collection of flowers
round robin (17C) a petition of protest whose signatures were originally arranged in a circle so that no name headed the list and no one person seemed to be the author (the robin does not refer to the bird but to the French *rond* for round and *ruban* for ribbon)
costume (18C) manners and customs belonging to a particular time and place

STICKYBEAK

Character

Let him that would be happy for a day,
go to the barber; for a week, marry a wife;
for a month, buy him a new horse; for a
year, build him a new house; for all his
life time, be an honest man

(1662)

According to legal statute an **idiot** is an individual with an IQ of less than 20, an **imbecile** between 21 and 49 and a **moron** between 50 and 70. As you cast around for insults it may be worth remembering these categories. But then again, the English language has never been short of slurs for the stupid. Historically, you could have been a **clumperton** (mid 16C), a **dull-pickle** or a **fopdoodle** (both 17C); and more recently, **two ants short of a picnic, two wafers short of a communion** or even **a few vouchers short of a pop-up toaster**.

Over the centuries, some other fine reproaches have included:

doddypoll (1401) a hornless cow, hence a fool
jobbernowl (1599) a blockhead
slubberdegullion (1616) a dirty, wretched slob
goostrumnoodle (Cornwall 1871) a stupid person, a fool

LOOSE KANGAROOS

Australians, in particular, specialize in scorn for the intellectually challenged. In the 1950s you could have been as **mad** (or **silly**) as a **cut snake**, a **hatful of worms** or a **Woolworth's watch**. More recently, in the 1980s, you might have been a **couple of tinnies short of a slab** or a **few snags short of a barbie** (where a **tinnie** is a beer can, a **slab** is a stack of cans and a **snag** is a sausage). Then again, a real idiot or **drongo** couldn't **blow the froth off a glass of beer, knock the skin off a rice-pudding**, **pick a seat at the pictures, find a grand piano in a one-roomed house**, or **tell the time if the town-hall clock fell on them**. Other memorable expressions of Antipodean scorn include **there's a kangaroo loose in the top paddock** and **the wheel is turning, but the hamster is dead**.

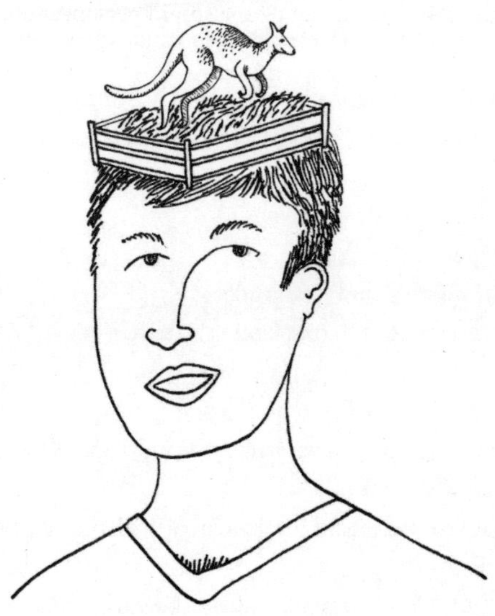

MEN OF STRAW

Fools can often be enthusiastic in their idiocy. Arguably more irritating are those whose marbles are all present, but who somehow just lack the drive:

dardledumdue (Norfolk 1893) a person without energy
maulifuff (Scotland) a young woman who makes a lot of fuss but accomplishes very little
gongoozler (1904) an idle person who stands staring for prolonged periods at anything unusual
mulligrubs (1599) a state of depression of spirits
accidie (Old French *c.*1230) spiritual torpor, world weariness

WHAT NOW?

Other types it's as well to steer clear of include the mean ...

chinchin (Middle English 1100–1500) to be stingy
stiff (hotel trade jargon) any customer that fails to leave a tip

the moaning ...

crusty-gripes (1887) a grumbler
choowow (Fife) to grumble, a grudge
forplaint (1423) tired by complaining so much

the nosey ...

quidnunc (1709) a person who always wants to know what is going on (from Latin: 'what now')
stickybeak (New Zealand 1937) an inquisitive person; also the nose of a nosy-parker
pysmatic (1652) interrogatory, always asking questions or inquiring

the elusive . . .

didapper (1612) someone who disappears and then pops up again
whiffler (1659) one who uses shifts and evasions in argument
kinshens (Scotland 1870) an evasive answer: 'I don't know, I cannot tell'
salt one up (US slang) to tell a different lie when covering up something
salvo (1659) a false excuse; an expedient to save a reputation or soothe hurt feelings

the unattractive . . .

farouche (Horace Walpole 1765) sullen, shy and repellent in manner
yahoo (Swift: *Gulliver's Travels* 1726) a crude or brutish person
ramstamphish (Scotland 1821) rough, blunt, unceremonious; forward and noisy

the tedious . . .

meh (US slang popularized by *The Simpsons*) boring, apathetic or unimpressive
whennie (UK current slang) a person who bores listeners with tales of past exploits

and the just plain impossible . . .

quisquous (Scotland 1720) hard to handle, ticklish
utzy (LA slang 1989) uncomfortable, bothered, uneasy
argol-bargolous (1822) quarrelsome, contentious about trifles
camstroudgeous (Fife) wild, unmanageable, obstinate, perverse
whiffling (1613) trifling, pettifogging, fiddling

TWO GENTLEMEN

In the early nineteenth century two gentlemen in particular were to be avoided. Though both types persist, social developments may mean we may see more of the second than the first these days. **A gentleman of three ins** was 'in gaol, indicted, and in danger of being hanged in chains'. While **a gentleman of three outs** was 'without money, without wit, and without manners'.

HIGH HAT

Foppish, conceited behaviour – once known as **coxcombical** (1716) – seems too to be a persistently male trait:

jackanapes (Northern 1839) a conceited, affected, puppyish young man
princock (1540) a pert, forward, saucy boy; a conceited young man
flapadosha (Yorkshire) an eccentric, showy person with superficial manners

WITCH'S BROOM

Women, by contrast, have come in for all kinds of criticism:

mackabroin (1546) a hideous old woman
Xanthippe (1596) an ill-tempered woman, a shrew (after Socrates's wife)
cantlax (Westmoreland) a silly, giddy woman
termagant (1659) a violent, brawling, quarrelsome woman
bungo-bessy (Jamaican 1940) a woman whose busybody qualities are considered highly undesirable
criss-miss (West Indian 1950s) a pretentious woman who overestimates her abilities, charms and allure

YUPPIES

Everyone's so used to the word yuppie now that they forget that only twenty-five years ago it was a brand new acronym for Young Urban Professional. Here are some other acronyms coined subsequently to that famous first:

SPURMO a Straight, Proud, Unmarried Man Over 30
SADFAB Single And Desperate For A Baby
CORGI a Couple Of Really Ghastly Individuals
SITCOM Single Income, Two Children, Oppressive Mortgage
KIPPERS Kids In Parental Property Eroding Retirement Savings
SKIERS Spending their Kids Inheritance (on travel, health and leisure activities)

SLYBOOTS

Better, perhaps, those who assume airs than those who seem straightforward but aren't:

janjansy (Cornwall 1888) a two-faced person
accismus (Medieval Latin 1753) feigning lack of interest in something while actually desiring it
mouth-honour (G. B. Shaw: *Major Barbara* 1907) civility without sincerity
mawworm (1850) a hypocrite with delusions of sanctity
Podsnap (from the character in Dickens' *Our Mutual Friend* 1864) a complacent, self-satisfied person who refuses to face unpleasant facts
skilamalink (East London slang late 19C) secret, shady

REGULAR GUY

Such characters make one long for that remarkable thing: the straightforward, decent, or just thoroughly good person . . .

rumblegumption (Burns: letter 1787) common sense
pancreatic (1660) fully disciplined or exercised in mind, having a universal mastery of accomplishments
towardliness (1569) a good disposition towards something, willingness, promise, aptness to learn
Rhadamanthine (Thackeray: *Paris Sketchbook* 1840) strictly honest and just (Rhadamanthus, Zeus's half-human son, was made a judge of the souls of the dead due to his inflexible integrity)

. . . this is someone we all want to spend time with, and stay loyal to . . .

wine (Old English) a friend
bully (Geordie) a brother, comrade
bread-and-cheese friend (Sussex) a true friend as distinguished from a **cupboard-lover** (a personal attachment that appears to be motivated by love but stems from the hope of gain)

WORD JOURNEYS

amnesty (16C from Ancient Greek) forgetfulness, oblivion
nice (13C from Latin nescire: to be ignorant) foolish; then (14C) coy, shy; then (16C) fastidious, precise; then (18C) agreeable, delightful
obnoxious (16C from Latin) exposed to harm
generous (16C from Latin via Old French) nobly born

GOING POSTAL

Emotions

Be not too sad of thy sorrow,
of thy joy be not too glad

(c.1450)

Throughout the world the British were once famed for their stiff upper lip; but is this sort of imperturbability really no more than a paper-thin façade for some extremely strong feelings beneath?

ugsomeness (1440) loathing
jump salty (US slang 1996) to become angry
brain (Middle English 1100–1500) furious
throw sarcasm (Jamaican English 1835) to relieve one's emotions by speaking out about one's dislike for or sense of grievance against another
unbosom (1628) to disclose one's personal thoughts or feelings

HOPPING MAD

It's now generally agreed that it's better to let it all out than keep it in:

dudgeon (1597) a resentful anger (dudgeon was a wood used to make dagger hilts)
mumpish (1721) sullenly angry; depressed in spirits
wooden swearing (US slang b.1935) showing anger by acts of violence or roughness, as in knocking furniture about
go postal (US slang 1986) to lose your temper, behave with irrational violence, especially as a result of workplace stress (from a postal worker who killed fourteen fellow employees and wounded six before shooting himself)

JESUS WEPT

Tears, too, are regarded as a good thing these days. But it doesn't stop them sometimes making for a **kankedort** (Chaucer: *Troylus* 1374) an awkward situation:

gowl (*c.*1300) to weep bitterly or threateningly
skirllie-weeack (Banffshire) to cry with a shrill voice
grizzle (1842) to fret, sulk; to cry in a whining or whimpering fashion
sinsorg (Anglo-Saxon) perpetual grief
bubble (Geordie) to weep

BRING ME SUNSHINE

Luckily sunshine eventually follows rain. Words describing happiness offer fascinating barometers into history. For instance, the Old English word for joy, **dream,** also describes music and ecstasy – an intriguing view into the mind-frame of our ancestors . . .

froligozene (Tudor–Stuart) rejoice! be happy!
fleshment (Shakespeare: *King Lear* 1605) excitement from a first success
felicificability (1865) capacity for happiness
macarism (mid 19C) taking pleasure in another's joy
maffick (1900) to rejoice with an extravagant and boisterous public celebration
kef (1808) a state of voluptuous dreaminess, full of languid contentment (originally used to describe the effects of opium)

MAKE 'EM LAUGH

We can't all be a **grinagog** (1565), one who is always grinning. But the contrast is all the better when we do finally get to see the funny side:

cachinnate (1824) to laugh loudly and immoderately
winnick (Lincolnshire) to giggle and laugh alternatively
snirtle (1785) to laugh in a quiet or restrained manner
popjoy (1853) to amuse oneself
goistering (Sussex) loud feminine laughter

HA HA BONK

Humour is often cruel. At the heart of slapstick are a series of jokes that amuse only those who set them up:

press ham (US college slang 1950s) to press a bare buttock against a window and shock passers-by

squelch-belch (Winchester College 1920) a paper bag of water dropped from an upper window onto people below

to catch the owl (late 18C) to play a trick on an innocent countryman, who is decoyed into a barn under the pretext of catching an owl: when he enters, a bucket of water is poured on his head

tiddley-bumpin' (Lincolnshire) tapping on a window pane with a button on a length of cotton secured to the frame by a pin (a device used by boys to annoy neighbours)

pigeon's milk (1777) an imaginary article for which children are sent on a fool's errand (traditionally on April 1st)

squashed tomatoes (1950s) a game that involves knocking on a door and then rushing away as the homeowner answers it (also known as **knock down ginger** (England and Canada), **ding-dong ditch** (US), **chappy** (Scotland), **dolly knock** (Ireland)

WORD JOURNEYS

jest (13C from Latin and French) a deed or exploit; then (15C) idle talk

engine (13C from Latin via Old French) contrivance, artifice; then (14C) genius

frantic (14C) insane

negotiate (16C from Latin) ill at ease; not at leisure

to have a chip on one's shoulder (US 19C) of a custom in which a boy who wanted to give vent to his feelings placed a chip of wood on his shoulder in order to challenge any boy who dared to knock it off

TWIDDLE-DIDDLES

Body language

Keep the head and feet warm,
and the rest will take nae harm

(1832)

In the developed world these days, one of the greatest concerns is being overweight, whether you are an adult or a child. But the evidence of language is that not being thin is hardly a new thing. Nor are people's reactions:

fubsy (1780) being chubby and somewhat squat
flodge (Banffshire) a big, fat, awkward person
ploffy (Cornwall 1846) plump; also soft and spongy
pursy (Scotland) short-breathed and fat
fustilug (1607) a fat sloppy woman
five by five (North American black 1930s) a short fat man (i.e. his girth is the same as his height)

CHUBBY CHOPS

It's not just the whole but the parts that get labelled. In the UK people talk about **bingo wings** for flabby upper arms, a **muffin top** to describe that unsightly roll of flesh above tight jeans, a **buffalo hump** for an area of fat in the upper back and **cankles** for ankles so thick that they have no distinction from the calf. Over the pond recent slang is just as critical:

bat wings flabby undersides of the upper arms
banana fold fat below the buttocks
chubb fat around the kneecaps
hail damage cellulite (from its pitted similarity to the effects of hail)

MODEL FIGURES

So it must be reassuring to some that being skinny can also attract unfavourable notice (especially when combined with height):

windlestraw (1818) a thin, lanky person
straight up six o'clock girl (US black 1940s) a thin woman
slindgy (Yorkshire 1897) tall, gaunt and sinewy
gammerstang (1570) a tall, awkward woman
stridewallops (Yorkshire) a tall, long-legged girl
flacket (Suffolk) a girl, tall and slender, who flounces about in loose hanging clothes

NAPOLEON COMPLEX

The awful truth is that from the playground onwards, people who don't meet the average have always had to put up with mockery. Luckily, vertically challenged role models from Alexander the Great to Napoleon have often had the last laugh:

youfat (Ayrshire 1821) diminutive, puny
gudget (Donegal) a short thick-set man
dobbet (Cornwall) a short, stumpy little person
pyknic (1925) short and squat in build, with small hands and feet, short limbs and neck, a round face and a domed abdomen
endomorphic (1888) being short but powerful

NIP AND TUCK

So in the short term what can you do to change things? Wear platform shoes. Go on a diet. Or consider having some 'work' done:

pumping party (Miami slang 2003) illegal gatherings where plastic surgeons give back street injections of silicone, botox, etc.

rhytidectomy (1931) the surgical removal of facial wrinkles

roider (US slang 2005) someone who injects illegal steroids to enhance his body

reveal party (US current slang) a party held to celebrate successful cosmetic treatment, especially cosmetic surgery or dentistry

MAKEOVER

Then again, you could just pop down to the salon and have a less final and painful sort of revamp:

whiffle cut a very short haircut worn by US soldiers in the Second World War

farmer's haircut (US slang 1984) a short haircut that leaves a white strip of skin showing between the bottom of the hair and the tanned portion of the neck

follow-me-lads (mid 19C) curls that hang over a woman's shoulder

krobylos (Ancient Greek 1850) a tuft of hair on top of one's head

acersecomic (1612) one whose hair has never been cut

FACE FUNGUS

Ever since William the Conqueror passed a law against beards, facial hair has gone in and out of fashion. After the return of the heroic soldiers from the Crimea in the 1850s, the hirsute look became wildly popular:

dundrearies (1858) a pair of whiskers that, cut sideways from the chin, are grown as long as possible (named after the comic character Lord Dundreary in the popular Victorian play *Our American Cousin*; these excessive sidechops, popular with gentlemen perambulating the centre of the capital, were also known as **Piccadilly Weepers**)

burke (*c.*1870) to dye one's moustache

bostruchizer (Oxford University *c.*1870) a small comb for curling the whiskers

THREADBARE

From **five o'clock stubble** to the **pudding ring** (Florida slang), a facial decoration made up of a moustache and a goatee, many men cherish their beards because it's the only kind of hair they have left:

pilgarlic (1529) a bald man (referring to a peeled head of garlic)
skating rink (US current slang) a bald head
egg-shell blonde (New Zealand 1949) a bald man

Better such terms as these than being fingered for having a **brillo** (UK playground slang), a merciless expression for the style of a middle-aged male who is attempting to fluff-up every hair to disguise his ever-expanding pate.

SNIFFER

Hair can do only so much to frame a face. You can't escape the features you've been given, especially that one in the middle:

simous (1634) having a very flat nose or with the end turned up
proboscidiform (1837) having a nose like an elephant's trunk
macrosmatic (1890) having a supersensitive nose
meldrop (*c.*1480) a drop of mucus at the end of the nose

A WORD IN YOUR SHELL-LIKE

Even the highest in the land have to learn to live with the particular shape of their auditory nerves:

FA Cup (UK playground slang 1990s) a person with protruding ears
latch-lug't (Cumberland) having ears which hang down instead of standing erect
sowl (Tudor–Stuart 1607) to pull by the ears

PEEPERS

Eyes are more than mere features, they are extraordinary organs we should do our very best to look after:

saccade (French 1953) the rapid jump made by the eye as it shifts from one object to another
canthus (Latin 1646) the angle between the eyelids at the corner of the eye
eyes in two watches (Royal Navy slang) of someone whose eyes appear to be moving independently of each other as a result of drunkenness or tiredness or both

especially if there's only one of them . . .

half-a-surprise (UK slang late 19C) a single black eye
seven-sided animal (18C riddle) a person with only one eye (they have a right side and a left side, a foreside and a backside, an outside, an inside and a blind side)

CAKE HOLE

The **glabella** (Latin 1598) is the gap between the eyebrows, and the **philtrum** (Latin 17C) the groove below the nose. But though the mouth below attracts such crude names as **gob**, **gash** and **kisser**, its features and actions are more delicately described:

wikins (Lincolnshire) the corners of the mouth
fipple (Scottish and Northern) the lower lip
fissilingual (b.1913) having a forked tongue
bivver (Gloucestershire) to quiver one's lips
mimp (1786) to speak in a prissy manner usually with pursed lips

GNASHERS

An evocative Australian expression describes **teeth like a row of condemned houses**. In this state, the only cure is to have them out and replaced with **graveyard chompers,** a Down Under phrase for false teeth, intriguingly similar to the Service slang **dead man's effects**. But dental problems persist from the earliest night-time cries onwards:

neg (Cornwall 1854) a baby's tooth
shoul (Shropshire) to shed the first teeth
laser lips; **metal mouth**; **tin grin** (US campus slang 1970s) a wearer of braces
gubbertushed (1621) having projecting teeth
snag (Gloucestershire) a tooth standing alone

CHEEK BY JOWL

What face would be complete without all those interesting bits in between?

joblocks (Shropshire) fleshy, hanging cheeks
bucculent (1656) fat-cheeked and wide-mouthed
pogonion (1897) the most projecting part of the midline of the chin
prognathous (1836) having a jaw which extends past the rest of one's face

. . . not to mention other decorative surface additions:

push (Tudor–Stuart) a pimple
turkey eggs (Lincolnshire) freckles
christened by the baker (late 18C) freckle-faced

BOTTLING IT

Having broad shoulders has generally been seen to be a good thing, both literally and metaphorically. Other shapes are for some reason considered less reliable:

bible-backed (1857) round-shouldered, like one who is always poring over a book
champagne shoulders (*c.*1860) sloping shoulders (from the likeness to the bottle's shape)
Coke-bottle shoulders (Royal Navy slang) shoulders possessed by those individuals who are unwilling to take responsibility in any matter (after its rounded shape)

SINISTER

Most of us are right-handed. Once again, it's the odd ones out who get noticed, and not kindly. Left-handed people have been variously described as **molly-dukered**, **corrie-fisted** and **skerry-handit** (Scotland); **car-handed**, **cack-handed** and **cowie-handed** (North East); **kay-fisted**, **kibbo**, **key-pawed** and **caggy-ont** (Lancashire); **cuddy-wifter** (Northumbria); **kay-neeaved** or **dolly-posh** (Yorkshire); **keggy** (East Midlands) and **Marlborough-handed** (Wiltshire); while **awk** (1440) is an old English word which means 'with or from the left hand' and thus the wrong way, backhanded, perverse or clumsy (hence awkward).

PAWS

But all hands are carefully observed, both for how they are and for what they're doing:

pugil (1576) what is carried between the thumb and two first fingers
yepsen (14C) as much as the cupped hands will hold
gowpins (Yorkshire) the two hands full when held together
quobbled (Wiltshire) of a woman's hands: shrivelled and wrinkled from being too long in the washtub
clumpst (1388) of hands stiff with cold (hence clumsy)
rope-hooky (UK nautical jargon late 19C) with fingers curled in (from years of handling ropes)

. . . right down to the detail of specific digits:

lik-pot (Middle English 1100–1500) the forefinger of the right hand
mercurial finger (Tudor–Stuart) the little finger (as in palmistry it was assigned to Mercury)
flesh-spades (Fielding: *Tom Jones* 1749) fingernails
gifts (UK slang b.1811) small white specks under the fingernails, said to portend gifts or presents
lirp (1548) to snap one's fingers
fillip (1543) a jerk of the finger let go from the thumb
vig (Somerset) to rub a finger quickly and gently forwards and backwards

JOHN THOMAS

Further down are those parts often described as 'private', but subject also to any number of other euphemisms and nicknames:

twiddle-diddles (b.1811) testicles
melvin (US slang 1991) to grab by the testicles
be docked smack smooth (mid 18C) to have had one's penis amputated
merkin (1617) counterfeit hair for women's private parts
hinchinarfer (late 19C) a grumpy woman (i.e. 'inch-and-a-halfer' referring to the length of the disgruntled woman's husband's penis)

BUNS

The Ancient Greek-derived word **callipygian** (1646) has long been used to describe shapely buttocks, while in US slang **badonkadonk** indicates a bottom of exceptional quality and bounce. Unfortunately, rather more ubiquitous are displays of a less appealing kind:

working man's smile (US slang) a builders' bottom

LEGS ELEVEN

Below that, it's good to have shapely **stumps** and elegant **plates of meat**, whatever the individual components look like:

prayerbones (1900s) the knees
baker's knee (1784) a knee bent inwards (from carrying a heavy bread-basket on the right arm)
Sciapodous (1798) having feet large enough to be used as a sunshade to shelter the whole body
hallux (1831) a big toe

NOISES OFF

Cock-throppled (1617) describes one of those people whose Adam's apple is largely developed; **noop** (1818) is Scottish dialect for the sharp point of the elbow; and both **axilla** (1616) and **oxter** (1597) are names for the armpit. But perhaps the oddest words of all are those describing the noises that bodies can make:

yask (Shropshire) the sound made by a violent effort to get rid of something in the throat
plapper (Banffshire) to make a soft noise with the lips
borborygmus (1719) the rumbling, gurgling, growling sounds made by the stomach

WORD JOURNEYS

handsome (1435) easy to handle; then (1577) convenient; then (Samuel Johnson 1755) beautiful, with dignity
fathom (Old English) the span of one's outstretched arms
shampoo (18C from Hindi) to massage the limbs
complexion (from Latin) woven together; then (14C) the bodily constitution, the combination of the four humours
cold shoulder (Medieval French) from a chateau guest who was served a cold shoulder of beef or mutton instead of hot meat, as a not-so gentle hint that he had overstayed his welcome

PRICK-ME-DAINTY

Clothes

Under greasie clothes,
are oft found rare virtues

(1666)

Even if you're not, as the Australians say, **as flash as a rat with a gold tooth**, you can still make time to be well turned out:

prick-me-dainty (1529) one that is finicky about dress; a dandy (of either sex)
pavisand (Kipling: *Simple Simon* 1910) to flaunt opulent or expensive clothing or jewels in a peacock-like fashion
flamfew (1580) a gaudily dressed female, whose chief pleasure consists of dress
sashmaree (Yorkshire) an elderly female conspicuous for the quaintness of her finery

UNMENTIONABLES

Not that all clothes are inherently smart:

cover-slut (1639) a clean apron over a dirty dress
orphan collar (US b.1902) a collar unsuitable to the shirt with which it is worn
stilt (Lincolnshire) to pull down and re-knit the feet of worn stockings or socks if the legs are still good
coax (UK slang mid 18C) to hide a dirty or torn part of one's stocking in one's shoes
apple-catchers (Herefordshire) outsized knickers (as one could use them for harvesting apples)

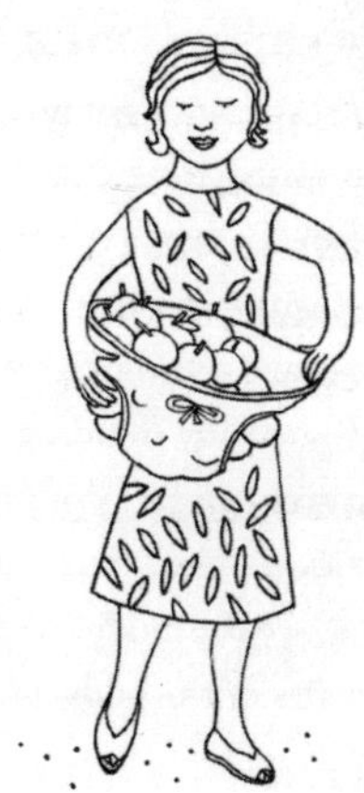

SKIMPIES

Garments that leave less to the imagination often attract greater interest:

banana hammock (US slang) a very brief men's swimsuit
pasties (strip club jargon 1961) coverings worn over the nipples of a showgirl's or topless dancer's breasts (to comply with legal requirements for entertainers)
budgie smugglers (Australian slang) tight-fitting swimming trunks

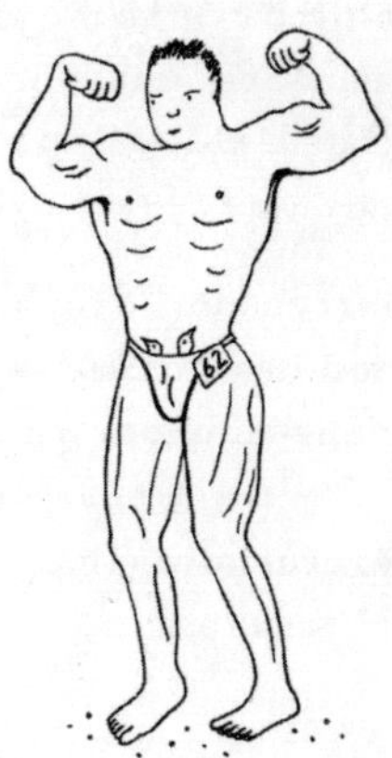

TREWS

But even slinging on a pair of trousers may not stop the ogling:

like Edgware Road (UK slang 20C) a phrase describing tight trousers (because it's got no ballroom either)
continuations (1825) trousers (since they continued a Victorian male's waistcoat in a direction too delicate to mention)
galligaskins (1577) loose breeches
spatterdashes (1687) coverings for the legs by which the wet is kept off (especially in riding)
gravity-bags (Westmorland) the seat of the trousers
yorks (Wales) the practice of tying colliers' and other workmen's trousers above the ankles to prevent dirt and dust from reaching the upper parts of the body

GYM SHOES

Here at home we mainly call them trainers these days. But around the country and the English-speaking world the slang varies widely. In Newcastle they're known as **sandshoes**; in Liverpool **gollies**; in Bristol and into Wales **daps**; in Nottingham **pumps**; in London **plimsolls**; in Dublin **whiteslippers**; and in Belfast **gutties**. Other types of footwear vary widely:

ferryboat (US 20C) a large, clumsy shoe
cod-heads (Glasgow 1930s) shoes that have worn out at the toe
done-promote (Jamaican English 1943) sandals made from worn out car tyres (i.e. one has been promoted from bare feet)
excruciators (19C) very tight, pointed shoes (forerunners of the 20C winklepickers)

KITTED OUT

Some occupations leave little choice as to what you wear:

lightning conductors (Royal Navy jargon) gold stripes running down the trouser seams of a Captain's or Flag Officer's Mess Dress uniform
devil's claw (*c*.1850) the broad arrow on convicts' uniform
fruit salad (Service slang) a large collection of medal ribbons which runs to three or more rows

SUITS YOU

There are all kinds of useful names for specific parts of clothing. Imagine how much easier life could be if you could define which pocket your keys are kept in or why exactly you have to turn down that fourth helping of turkey . . .

gerve (US late 19C) the breast-pocket in a jacket
britch (US late 19C) the inside jacket pocket
coppish (Glamorgan) the part of the trousers that have buttons in front
slave (US military slang) the part of a garment covering an arm only
yule-hole (Scots b.1911) the last hole to which a man could stretch his belt at a Christmas feast

REBELS IN BOATERS

Boys at Winchester College developed a rich lingo to describe how they wore their uniform. You could **sport** . . .

a fringe (1920) to allow the bottom of one's gown to become tattered
an advertisement (1892) to turn down the collar of a College gown to show the velvet
an angle (1920) to wear your straw hat crooked

Or more precisely:

a halo (1920) to have your hat tilted like a halo so that the hair was showing in front

PERUKE

Looking round at all the shaven heads and brillos of today, perhaps men should consider a return to something that was once an essential accessory, even if the language used to describe it was somewhat less than heroic:

cauliflower (1753) a large white wig, such as is worn by the dignified clergy and formerly by physicians
dildo (1688) a cylindrical or 'sausage' curl on a wig
caxon (1756) a worn-out wig
Nazarene foretop (1785) the foretop of a wig made in imitation of Christ's head of hair, as represented by the painters and sculptors

TOPPING

Or else, fly in the face of contemporary fashion and sport some other headgear:

liripipe (1737) the long tail of a graduate's hood
cow's breakfast (Canadian slang) a large straw hat
gibus (1848) an opera or crush hat
havelock (1861) a cloth hanging from the back of a soldier's cap to protect his neck from the sun
biggin (1530) a tight-fitting cap tied under the chin, usually worn by children or as a nightcap by men
goodgodster (Winchester College 1920) a brown bowler hat (from the exclamation necessarily uttered by anyone seeing so strange a thing)

WORD JOURNEYS

corset (14C from Latin and Old French) a little body

mitten (14C from Old French) divided in the middle

garter (14C from Old French) the bend in the knee

tuxedo (from Amerindian) a wolf; then the name of a lake near New York whose residents in 1886 became so socially important that its name was given to a new style of dinner coats

GOING WEST

Illness, death and spiritual matters

Sickness doth wound or afflict the flesh,
but it cures the soule

(1624)

The idealized body is all very well to look at, in a painting or beautiful photograph. But in life, of course, bodies are constantly working organisms, managing repetitive functions that we often try and pretend are not actually happening to us. Just look at the string of euphemisms for our regular trips to the loo or restroom. We **go and check the price of wheat in Chicago** (Fife), **see the vicar and book a seat for evensong** (Isle of Wight), **shake the dew from one's orchid** (Cumbria) or **wring out one's socks** (Kent).

WIND AND WATER

Related functions can cause us huge embarrassment, as we attempt to ignore the fact that air needs to be released or that sometimes the body will reject what we try and put into it:

fluff (Yorkshire) to break wind silently
dumb insolence (1916) breaking wind on parade
thorough cough (b.1811) coughing and breaking wind backwards at the same time
bespawl (Tudor–Stuart) to bespatter with saliva
vurp (UK teen talk) a belching action that's somewhere between vomiting and burping
bake it (late 19C) to refrain from visiting the loo when one should go there

ELF WARNING

Nor, sadly, can we rely on the body always to be in tip-top condition:

phthisickin (Essex) a slight, tickling cough
waff (1808) just the slightest touch of illness (especially of a cold)
aelfsogooa (Anglo-Saxon) a hiccough, thought to have been caused by elves
blepharospasm (1872) uncontrollable winking
galea (1854) a headache which covers the entire head like a helmet
mubble-fubbles (1589) a fit of depression
sirkenton (Ayrshire) one who is very careful to avoid pain or cold and keeps near the fire

MENS SANA

Though sometimes malfunction of the body has more to do with the mind that controls it . . .

formication (1707) the sensation of bugs crawling over one's body
trichotillomania (1889) the compulsive desire to pull out one's hair
boanthropy (1864) the belief that one is an ox
uranomania (1890) the delusion that one is of Heavenly descent
calenture (1593) a distemper peculiar to sailors in hot climates, where they imagine the sea to be green fields, and will throw themselves into it

DOCTOR IN THE HOUSE

Calling in professional assistance is sure to be a good plan, even if the treatment prescribed may sometimes seem a bit unusual:

urtication (1837) the act of whipping a palsied or benumbed limb with nettles to restore its feeling
bezoar (1580) a stone from a goat's stomach considered a universal antidote to poisons
organ recital (medical jargon) a detailing of one's medical history (especially of a hypochondriac's)
emporiatrics (medical terminology) the science of travellers' health (jet lag, exotic infections, overexposure to hot or cold, altitude sickness etc.)

GOD KNOWS

Irreverent medical acronyms are used by some doctors on patients' charts:

UBI Unexplained Beer Injury
PAFO Pissed And Fell Over
GORK God Only Really Knows (a hospital patient who is, and may well remain, comatose)
TEETH Tried Everything Else, Try Homeopathy
GPO Good for Parts Only

There is even a rumour that certain medics use the letters **O** and **Q** to describe their very oldest patients, with respectively, their mouths open, and their tongues out.

PULLING THROUGH

The sad fact remains that in the lottery of illness, some are fortunate . . .

umbersorrow (Scotland) hardy, resisting disease or the effects of severe weather
lysis (1877) the gradual reduction of the symptoms of a disease
to cheat the worms (b.1887) to recover from a serious illness
creaking gate (1854) an invalid who outlives an apparently healthier person (as a creaking gate hangs longest on the hinges)

. . . while others are less so (whatever their visitors think):

goodly-badly (Cumberland) of a sick person whose looks belie their illness
floccillation (1842) the action of a feverish patient in picking at the bedclothes during delirium
churchyard cough (1693) a cough that is likely to terminate in death
circling the drain (hospital jargon) a patient near death who refuses to give up the ghost
wag-at-the-wall (Jamaican English) a ghost that haunts the kitchen and moves backwards and forwards before the death of one of the family

LAST WORDS

Your time has come, and this is a journey with no return ticket:

thanatopsis (1816) the contemplation of death
viaticum (Latin 1562) Holy Communion given to a dying person
thratch (Scotland 1806) to gasp convulsively in the death-agony
dormition (1483) a peaceful and painless death

THE GOLDEN STAIRCASE

This final action of the body is also something that people prefer not to refer to directly, as the following euphemisms for dying attest:

buy the farm (US slang early 1900s)
climb the golden staircase (US slang late 1800s)
coil up one's ropes (British naval slang)
stick one's spoon in the wall (British slang 1800s)
meet one's Waterloo (Australian slang)
go trumpet-cleaning (late 19C: the trumpeter being the angel Gabriel)
chuck seven (late 19C: as a dice-cube has no 7)
drop one's leaf (*c.*1820)
take the everlasting knock (1889)
pass in one's cheeks (b.1872)

DEATH BY HONEY

Not of course that illness is the only way to go:

buddle (Somerset) to suffocate in mud
burke (1829) to smother people in order to sell their bodies for dissection (after the notorious Edinburgh body-snatchers Burke and Hare)
scaphism (b.1913) an old Persian method of executing criminals by covering them with honey and letting the sun and the insects finish the job

A HEARTY JOKE

When hanging was the ultimate penalty in this country, as it was for many centuries, a particular kind of gloating black humour went along with the licensed murder of wicked people:

hemp cravat (late 18C) a hangman's noose
to cry cockles (b.1811) to be hanged (from the noise made whilst strangling)
artichoke (underworld slang 1834) a hanging (a 'hearty choke')
horse's nightcap (late 18C) the cap drawn over a criminal's eyes at his hanging (also known as **Paddington spectacles** (early 19C) from the execution of malefactors at Tyburn in the above parish)
keep an ironmonger's shop by the side of a common (1780) to be hanged in chains
sheriff's picture frame (UK slang b.1811) the gallows
dismal ditty (*c.*1690) a psalm sung by a criminal just before his death at the gallows

DUST TO DUST

However you meet your end, it's off to church for one last time:

ecopod (UK 1994) a coffin specially designed to be environmentally friendly
shillibeer (1835) a hearse with seats for mourners
wheelicruise (Orkney Isles dialect) a churchyard
boot hill (American West 19C) a graveyard (where the occupants died 'with their boots on' i.e. violently)
parentate (1620) to celebrate one's parents' funerals

KNOCKING-ON

Not that death is necessarily the end of your consequence on earth:

dustsceawung (Anglo-Saxon) a visit to a grave ('a viewing of dust')
carrion-crow man (Guyanese English) a man who canvasses business for an undertaker following a death
umest (1400) the coverlet of a bed, often claimed by a priest at the death of a parishioner
to add a stone to someone's cairn (18C) to honour a person as much as possible after their death
memorial diamond (US slang 2001) a diamond created from carbon extracted from the remains of a cremated body
deodand (1523) an object that has been the direct cause of death of a human being (such as a boat from which a person has fallen and drowned) which was forfeited to the crown to be used as an offering to God

ELYSIAN FIELDS

The spirit has most definitely left the body, but to travel who knows where? Over the centuries there have been many different answers to this fascinating question:

fiddlers' green (1825) the place where sailors expect to go when they die: a place of fiddling, dancing, rum and tobacco

psychopannychy (1545) the sleep of the soul between death and the day of judgment

Lubberland (1598) a mythical paradise reserved for those who are lazy

GOD'S IN HIS HEAVEN

Back on earth, those left behind try and make sense of this alarming flight. Many find a visit to a church helpful in all kinds of ways . . .

scaldabanco (1670) a preacher who delivers a fiery sermon
utraquist (1894) one who partakes of the wine as well as the bread at communion
officers of the 52nd (b.1909) young men rigidly going to church on the 52 Sundays in a year

. . . though some motives are more suspect than others:

thorough churchman (b.1811) a person who goes in at one door of a church, and out at the other without stopping
autem-diver (17C) a pickpocket specializing in the robbery of church congregations

SPEAK OF THE DEVIL

God is known by few names: God, Allah, Jehovah. But his old adversary has any number of monikers: **author of evil**, **black gentleman**, **fallen angel**, **old scratch**, **old split-foot** and **the noseless one**. Just in the north-east of England he's been **Clootie**, **Awd Horney**, **Auld Nick** and the **Bad Man**, while Yorkshire has had him as **Dicky Devlin**; Gloucestershire as **Miffy** and Suffolk as **Jack-a-Dells**.

THE UNCERTAIN FUTURE

Religion asks us to accept our fate, whatever that may be. For many that's not good enough. They need more concrete assurance of the good or bad things to come:

onychomancy (1652) fortune-telling using reflected light on oiled fingernails

pessomancy (1727) divination by throwing pebbles

belomancy (1646) divination using arrows marked with symbols or questions, guidance being sought by firing the arrows or drawing them at random from a bag or quiver

planchette (French 1920s) a small, heart-shaped board on casters with a pencil attached; when participants in a séance touched it lightly the planchette allegedly wrote messages from the dead

WORD JOURNEYS

juggernaut (17C) from Hindi jagannath: a title of the god Vishnu 'lord of the world'. It was believed that devotees of Vishnu threw themselves beneath the wheels of a cart bearing his image in procession

mortgage (14C from Old French) a death pledge, a promise to pay upon a person's death

bask (14C) to bathe in blood

bless (Old English) to redden with blood; then to consecrate

SLAPSAUCE
Food

An apple pie without the cheese is like
the kiss without the squeeze

(1929)

British food is often unfavourably compared with the cuisines of other nations. But why on earth should this be?

dribble-beards (Scotland 1829) long strips of cabbage in broth
dog and maggot (UK military forces) biscuits and cheese
chussha-wagga (Worcestershire) inferior cheese
druschoch (Ayrshire) any liquid food of a nauseating appearance

HORSE FODDER

Dr Johnson famously described oats as 'a grain which is in England given to horses, but in Scotland supports the people'. Turnips on the other hand have long sustained people on both sides of the border. In the dialect of north-east England they have been known as **bagies**, **naggies**, **narkies**, **nashers**, **snadgers**, **snaggers**, **snannies**, **snarters**, **tungies** and **yammies**. In Scotland they're called **neeps**, as in **bashed neeps** (mashed turnips) the traditional accompaniment to haggis.

KITCHEN CONFIDENTIAL

Pig-months (19C) are those months in the year which have an 'r' in their name: that is, all except the summer months of May, June, July or August, when it was traditionally considered unwise to eat pork (or shellfish). But however safe your ingredients, correct preparation is essential:

spitchcock (1675) to prepare an eel for the table
bonx (Essex) to beat up batter for pudding
engastration (1814) the act of stuffing one bird into another (the result is called a **turducken**)
sclench (Shropshire) to check water at its boiling point, by dashing cold water into it
swinge (Newfoundland 1896) to burn the down off sea-birds after plucking the feathers

CAT'S PRAYERS

Fancy names abound for different types of food, whether they be barely edible, plain or thought of as a delicacy:

Boston strawberries (US late 19C) baked beans

call-dog (Jamaican English 1943) a fish too small for human consumption (so one calls the dog to eat it)

first lady (US drugstore jargon 1930s) spare ribs (Eve was made from Adam's rib)

scuttle-mouth (1848) a small oyster in a very large shell

pishpash (Anglo-Indian) a slop of rice-soup with small pieces of meat in it

bobby-jub (Yorkshire) strawberries and cream

dandyfunk (nautical jargon 1883) a ship's biscuit, soaked in water, mixed with fat and molasses, and baked in a pan

spadger (Tudor–Stuart) a sparrow; something small and tasty (sparrows were an Elizabethan delicacy)

armored cow (US army slang 1940s) canned milk

honeymoon salad (US diner jargon) lettuce alone (i.e. 'let us alone')

Adam and Eve on a raft (US diner jargon) two fried eggs on a piece of toast

GIVE AND TAKE AND EAT IT – RHYMING SLANG

Some rhyming slang simply rhymes but the best stuff takes it further, with meaning carried across:

borrow and beg (late 19C) an egg (the term enjoyed a fresh lease of life during the Second World War food-rationing period)
give and take (20C) cake (no cake can be eaten that has not been given)
satin and silk (American Pacific Coast 20C) milk (suggestive of this liquid food's smoothness)
army and navy (early 20C) gravy (which was plentiful at meal times in both services)
didn't ought (late 19C) port (based on the replies of ladies who, when asked to 'have another', said that they 'didn't ought')

PLUS ONE

Whatever you put on your table, you can be fairly sure that there'll be someone around to hoover it up:

smell-feast (1519) one who haunts good tables, a greedy sponger
cosherer (1634) someone who feasts or lives upon the industry of others
slapsauce (1573) a person who enjoys eating fine food, a glutton
hodger (US slang) a guest who eats all of the host's food and drinks all of the host's drinks

STOP PINGLING

Perhaps the best you can hope for is reasonable table manners:

dooadge (Yorkshire) to handle food in a messy way (often said of children)
mimp (1861) to play with one's food
pingle (Suffolk) to move food about on the plate for want of an appetite
sword swallower (Australian slang) someone eating from his knife, especially among shearers
yaffle (1788) to eat or drink especially noisily or greedily

. . . or at least guests who aren't fussy eaters:

pica (1563) a strong and unnatural craving for unsuitable food (such as chalk), which occurs during pregnancy
omophagist (1884) a person who eats raw flesh
pozzy-wallah (Tommies' slang 1914–18) a man inordinately fond of jam

POST-PRANDIAL

And then, hunger sated, you have the opportunity to sit back, digest and relax. Just keep an eye on all your guests . . .

rizzle (1890) to enjoy a short period of absolute idleness after a meal
nooningscaup (Yorkshire 18C) the labourer's resting time after dinner
dando (19C) one who frequents hotels, eating-houses and other such places, satisfies his appetite and decamps without payment

WORD JOURNEYS

omelette (17C from French via Latin) a thin flat blade
pittance (13C from Latin via Old French) originally a pious request; then (14C) donations to monastic orders on a person's death to be spent on food and wine to be served on the anniversary of the donor's death; then (16C) these diminished to the extent of meaning a sparing allowance
bulb (17C from Ancient Greek via Latin) an onion
companion (18C from Latin) someone who eats bread with you

CRAMBAZZLED
Drink

It's all right to drink like a fish
– if you drink what a fish drinks

(1938)

After your meal, what could be better than a cup of tea. Just make sure you've remembered to warm the pot and observe all the other niceties:

to drown the miller to put too much water into tea (the supply of water is so great that even the miller, who uses a water wheel, is drowned with it)

stranger (Sussex dialect) a single tea-leaf floating in a cup of tea

laptea (US slang) a crowded tea party where guests sit in each other's laps

to smash the teapot (late 19C) to abandon one's pledge of abstinence from alcohol (the symbolic rejection of tea as one's sole liquid stimulant)

DOWN AT THE OLD BULL AND BUSH

In Britain the drinking of alcohol has always been, for better or worse, at the heart of the community. The Romans had *tabernae* (the origin of our word tavern), which turned into the Anglo-Saxon alehouses, where a brewer would put a green bush up on a pole when the ale was ready to drink:

kiddleywink (1830) an unlicensed public house

build a sconce (18C) to run up a large bill at a tavern especially when one has no intention of paying

brendice (1673) a cup in which a person's health is drunk

spit chips (Australian slang 1901) extreme thirst (from the idea of having dry wood in your mouth)

flairing (Sydney slang) the action of bartenders of balancing, catching, flipping, spinning or throwing bottles, glasses, napkins or straws with finesse and style

MINE'S A NIPPITATUM

The traditional pint comes in many forms:

arms and legs (UK slang 19C) weak beer (i.e. a drink that has no body)

nippitatum (1576) exceptionally strong beer

barbed wire (Australian slang, Darwin) Four X beer (from the xxxx symbol)

parson's collar (1940s) the froth on top of a glass of beer

neckum, sinkum and **swankum** (Berkshire) the three draughts into which a jug of beer is divided

ON THE NAIL

Though for refined types more Continental beverages may be preferred, whatever their quality:

supernaculum (1592) the finest wine, which is so good it is drunk to the last drop, referring to the custom of turning over a drained glass and letting the last drop of wine fall onto the thumbnail (from the Latin 'upon the nail')

butler's perks (UK euphemism) opened but unfinished bottles of wine

beeswing (1860) the scum found on the surface of aged wine

balderdash (1611) adulterated wine

PEARLY GATES

The names of British pubs are not all that they seem – certainly if you're looking at the picture on the sign hanging outside them. **The Cat and Fiddle** didn't derive from a music-loving publican who kept cats, but is a corruption of Catherine le Fidèle, which refers to the faithfulness of Catherine of Aragon, Henry VIII's first wife. The **Hope and Anchor** comes from the Biblical text 'We have this as a sure and steadfast anchor of the soul, a hope'; **The Cross Keys** is the symbol of St Peter, the gatekeeper of heaven; and **The Royal Oak** commemorates the tree that hid Charles II from Oliver Cromwell's forces after his defeat at Worcester.

LAST GASPER

In Tudor times **drink** actually meant to smoke tobacco, something you could once do inside the bar. Now the **misocapnists** (1839), those who hate the smell of smoke, are in charge, so that's a pleasure restricted to the pavements outside:

smirting (US slang New York) flirting between people who are smoking cigarettes outside a pub, office etc.
vogueress (Polari slang) a female smoker
casablanca (Tommies' slang 1914–18) the last one, especially of cigarettes
doofer (workmen's slang b.1935) half a cigarette
toss the squares (US black slang) to pass a packet of cigarettes
whiffler (1617) a smoker of tobacco

JUST THE ONE

Take it or leave it, boozing is a serious business:

cagg (UK military slang b.1811) a solemn vow or resolution used by private soldiers not to get drunk for a certain time
parson palmer (late 18C) a term of reproach, to one who stops the decanter circulating by preaching over his liquor (as was done by a parson of that name whose cellar was under his pulpit)
duffifie (Aberdeenshire) to lay a bottle on its side for some time, after its contents have been poured out, so that it may be completely drained of the few drops remaining

SPEAKEASY

Just make sure your companions understand the importance of paying their way:

to raddle someone's toe (Australian late 19C) to request someone to buy a round of drinks
twizzling (Sussex) spinning a pointer on a pub ceiling to decide who should buy the next round
decorate the mahogany (Hobo slang) to buy the drinks; to line the bar with thirsty throats and brimming glasses
shot-clog (1599) an unwelcome drinking companion tolerated because he pays for the drinks

DRINK AND BE MERRY?

Soon, if you're not exactly **zig-zag** – Tommies' slang from the First World War for the state where it's impossible to walk in a straight line – the booze will certainly be making itself felt:

hozzy nozzy (Rutland) not quite drunk
bleezed (Scotland 19C) the state of one on whom intoxicating liquor begins to operate: especially describing the change produced in one's facial expression
cherubimical (Benjamin Franklin 1737) benevolently drunk
tenant in tail (mid 17C) one whose drunkenness promotes indiscriminate displays of affection
whiffled (P. G.Wodehouse: *Meet Mr Mulliner* 1927) drunk

FROM SHEEP TO SOW

In Lincolnshire they marked out four distinct phases of intoxication. A man was **sheep drunk** when he was merry and easily handled; then **lion drunk** when he was brave and boastful; **ape drunk** when he got up to silly, irresponsible tricks; and finally **sow drunk** when he fell to the ground in an alcoholic stupor.

TWO TOO MANY

Sailors are legendary for their drinking prowess but watch out for these two:

admiral of the narrow seas (early 17C) a drunkard who vomits over his neighbour

vice admiral of the narrow seas (1811) a drunken man that pisses under the table into his companions' shoes

THE MOURNING AFTER

Being drunk means never having to say you're sorry, until the next morning of course when you forswear alcohol for tea again:

take a sheep-bed (Wiltshire) to lie down like a sheep to sleep in a grass-field, till one is sober

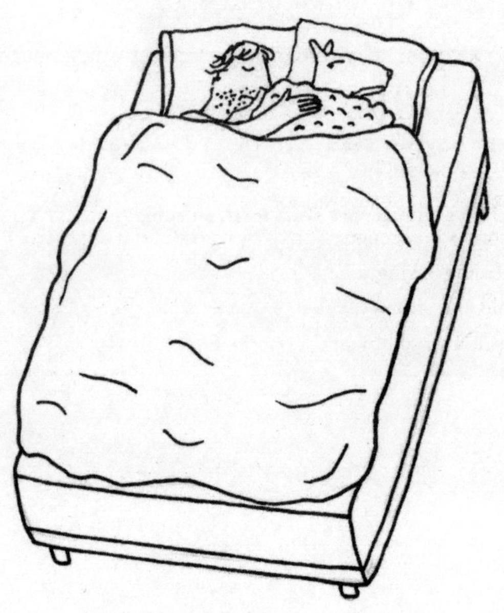

woofits (1918) a hangover; a vague unwell feeling; a headache; a moody depression

gunfire (Service slang) early morning tea (because it often has to be of considerable strength to counteract a bad head)

to feel as if a cat had kitten'd in one's mouth (16C) to feel the nauseous after-effects of drinking

crambazzled (Yorkshire) prematurely aged through drink and a dissolute life

WORD JOURNEYS

bonkers (early 20C) slightly tipsy

tobacconist (16C) a tobacco smoker

grape (11C from Old French) a hook for gathering fruit; then a cluster of fruit growing together

stale (13C) old and strong (applied to wine and ale having stood long enough to clear of sediment)

FOOTER-FOOTER

Taking off

A traveller must have the backe of an asse
to beare all, a tung like the taile of a dog to
flatter all, the mouth of a hogge to eate what
is set before him, the eare of a merchant
to heare all and say nothing

(1594)

Going for a walk is the quintessential English form of relaxation; but there are many varieties within the basic idea of putting one foot in front of another . . .

mantle (Lincolnshire) to walk aimlessly up and down with short steps
starp (North East) to walk with long strides
footer-footer (Scotland 1894) to walk in an affected mincing manner
nuddle (Suffolk) to walk alone with the head held low
slochet (Bedfordshire 1809) to walk with shoes nearly falling off the feet
festination (1878) walking faster and faster involuntarily

. . . and sometimes it can all seem a bit too much:

pouff (Banffshire) the act of walking with a heavy step, especially through weariness
plout (North East) to struggle to walk
surbater (1633) someone who tires another person out by walking
hox (Gloucestershire) to knock the feet together while walking
dot and go one (b.1811) to waddle: of people with one leg shorter than the other
darby-roll (19C) a style of walking that betrays an individual's experience of fetters and thus time spent in prison

BONE-BREAKER

So why not take up that efficient, ecological and highly fashionable way of getting around – just be sure not to flirt with its dangers:

croggie (UK school slang 2003) a ride of the crossbar or handlebars of another rider's bicycle

blackadder (West Scotland playground slang) the action of allowing a bike to continue its journey without a rider (usually performed at the top of hills on either old, borrowed or stolen bikes)

endo (US slang San Francisco 1987) a bicycling accident in which the rider is thrown over the handlebars

SMIDSY (cyclists' acronym) Sorry Mate, I Didn't See You

acrobrat (UK playground slang 1970s) a kid who attaches poles to the front axle of his bike so he can bounce up and down on the front wheel

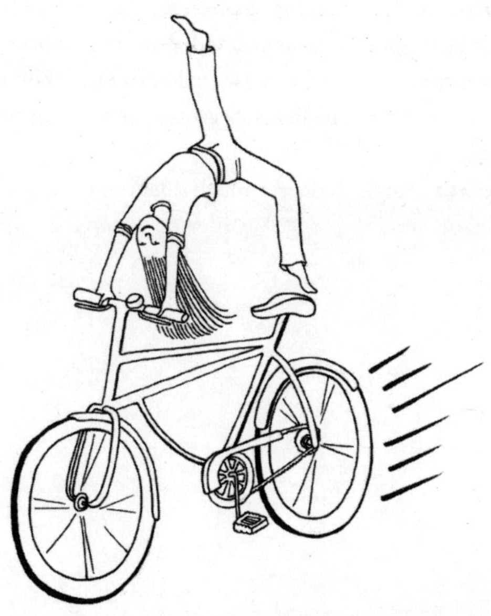

GO CART

Once upon a time more substantial vehicles moved slowly and with difficulty:

unicorn (1785) a coach drawn by three horses, two abreast and one in the lead

timwhisky (1764) a light carriage for one or two people, pulled by one or two horses

quarter (Shropshire) to drive a cart in a lane with deep ruts, in such a way as to keep each wheel clear of them

to hunt the squirrel (18C) for two coachmen to attempt to upset each other's vehicles as they race along a public road (veering from side to side like a frightened squirrel)

Now the opposite is too often the case:

garyboy (East Anglia slang 1995) a male who drives a car usually noticeable by its sporty appearance and souped up engine

swoop and squat (US slang 2005) to pull in front of another vehicle and slam on the brakes, deliberately causing an accident to collect the insurance money

chawbuckswar (Anglo-Indian) a rough rider

TICKET TO RIDE

Not that you need to have your own transport to get around:

fly canaries (underworld slang 1945) to pass off used tram tickets as new ones

monkey board (mid 19C) the step on the bus on which the conductor stands

hong! and **midor!** (UK transport workers' jargon) 'hurry along' and 'mind the doors'

Cinderella fare (US cabdrivers' slang) people left behind on the platform when the last train leaves late at night

I SPY

Travelling piquet (1785–1840) was one way bored travellers amused themselves when riding together in a carriage. Scores were given for people and objects passing by on their side of the carriage, as follows:

a man or woman walking = 1
a horseman = 2
a post chaise = 5
a flock of geese = 10
a flock of sheep = 20
a man with a woman behind him = 30
a man, woman and child, in a buggy = 40
a cat looking out of a window = 60
an old woman under a hedge = game won
a parson riding a grey horse with blue tack = game won

GRICER'S DAUGHTER

Let's not forget those who are happy just to watch. Trainspotters may be mocked by the outside world, but they don't take criticism lying down: the language of **gricing** is notable for its acidic descriptions of outsiders.

bert the majority of people on trains, only interested in getting from A to B

insects occasional railway enthusiasts who swarm at certain times of year

kettle basher someone obsessed with steam engines (looked on as an effete sentimentalist)

baglet a woman, generally looked upon with unfriendliness. Gricers are invariably male. Worst of all women is **The Baglet** – Lady Thatcher, whose reluctance to travel by train was legendary and who set the privatization of British Rail in progress

ELSEWHERE

Hopefully you will arrive safely at your destination. Though some places, traditionally, have been more euphemistic than real. You could **go to** ...

Jericho (late 18C) to become drunk
Bath (mid 17C) to take up life as a beggar
Chicago (US late 19C) to run away, especially to avoid one's debts
Copenhagen (1950s) to have a sex operation
the Bahamas (US slang) to be sent to solitary confinement
Peckham (early 19C) to sit down to eat

WORD JOURNEYS

muddle (17C) to wallow in mud
walk (from German) to press cloth, knead or roll paste; then (Old English) to roll, toss, move about
insult (16C from Latin) to leap upon; then (16C) to glory or triumph over
random (15C) great speed, violence; then (17C) of a shot: haphazard, without purpose, fired at any range other than point blank

MUTTONERS AND GOLDEN FERRETS

Sport

Sport is sweetest when
there be no lookers on

(1616)

Sport has always been a part of British national life. In the beginning were the informal games that anyone could play anywhere:

way-zaltin (Somerset) a game in which two persons standing back to back interlace each other's arms and by bending forward alternately raise each other from the ground

hot cockles (1580) a rustic game in which one player lay face downwards, or knelt down with his eyes covered, and being struck by the others in turn, guessed who struck him

hinch-pinch (1603) a game where one person hits another softly, then the other player hits back with a little more force, and each subsequent blow in turn is harder, until it becomes a real fight

IN TOUCH

Many of our best-known sports started life in similar fashion. The earliest games of football involved one village taking on another, in violent, day-long combats where broken legs and bruised heads were common. Current slang reveals that underneath, perhaps, little has changed:

blaggudy (Wales) rough, dirty (especially of a football or rugby team)
clogger (UK slang 1970) a soccer player who regularly injures other players
sprig-stomping (New Zealand 1993) the deliberate stamping with studded boots on a recumbent rugby opponent
falling leaf a long-range shot in football which sees the ball change direction radically in the course of its flight
spaghetti-legs routine a goalkeeper's trick employed to distract a penalty taker

SECONDS AWAY

Another of our oldest sports had similar rough-and-tumble beginnings:

clow (Winchester 19C) a box on the ear
glass jaw (US slang 1940) of a boxer with an inability to withstand a punch to the chin
haymaker (1912) an unrestrained punch usually leading to a knockout, whereby the fist is swung wide in an arc
claret christening (b.1923) the first blood that flows in a boxing match
waterboy (US police slang 1930s) a boxer who can be bribed or coerced into losing for gambling purposes

FROM LAND'S END TO BROADWAY

Wrestling, too, has become less violent and more theatrical over the years, with a terminology that dates back to its origins, supplemented by more recent slang from around the world ...

falx (Tudor–Stuart) a grip round the small of the back
Cornish hug a hug that causes one to be thrown over (Cornish men were famous wrestlers)
sugarbagging the tossing of an opponent onto the canvas as if he were a bag of sugar
whizzer an arm lock trapping one's arm against the opponent's body from a position behind him

potato (US slang 1990) a real hit that injures, as opposed to an orchestrated, harmless one

jobber a wrestler whose primary function is losing to better-known wrestlers

broadway a drawn result (so-called because, ideally, the result makes both men bigger stars)

OVER AND OUT

Another quintessentially English game has a host of extraordinary terms, from the **yorker** (a ball pitched directly at the batsman's feet) to **silly mid-off** (a fielding position close to and in front of the batsman). Other words have fallen out of fashion:

muttoner (Winchester College 1831) a blow from a cricket ball on the knuckles, the bat being at the time clasped by them

slobber (1851) to fail to grasp the cricket ball cleanly in fielding

bowl a gallon (Eton College *c.*1860) to get a hat-trick (the bowler then earned a gallon of beer)

TO THE 19TH

For the more senior sportsman, another gentler but equally demanding game with British (well Scottish, strictly) roots has been successfully exported around the world. First comes the teeing off, with all the problems that that entails:

waggle pre-stroke trial movements
sclaffing skidding the club over the grass before it hits the ball
whiff a stroke that misses the ball
skull to hit the ball too far above its centre
shank to hit the ball with the neck of the club

then the slow or fast progression down the fairway:

chilli-dip a weak, lofted shot that follows a mis-hit that has managed to hit more ground than ball (from the image of taking a taco and scooping up a helping of chilli)
fried egg a ball lying embedded in sand
golden ferret a golf stroke where the ball is holed from a bunker
mulligan a free extra shot sometimes taken as a second chance in a social match to a player who has made a bad one, not counted on his score-card

before the triumphant arrival at the green:

frog hair the well-cut grass that divides the fairway from the green itself and is of a length and smoothness somewhere between the two
steamy a short shot or a putt that passes over or through the green
stiff a shot that stops so close to the hole that it must be impossible to miss the putt

TOUCHÉ

Fencing, by contrast to all of the above, originated on the Continent and so has a language with a very European feel:

mandritta (Tudor–Stuart 1595) a cut from right to left
passado (Shakespeare: *Love's Labour's Lost* 1588) a motion forwards and a thrust
volt (1692) to leap with both feet in the air by your opponent's left shoulder
appel a tap or stamp of the foot, serving as a warning of one's intent to attack
derobement an evasion of the opponent's attempt to take or beat the blade while keeping the sword arm straight and threatening the opponent

TOUR DE FRANCE

Since their invention in France in 1860, bicycles have been eagerly embraced by our Gallic neighbours. So it's hardly surprising that cycling is a sport with a French-derived argot:

musette a small cotton shoulder bag containing food that's handed to riders during a race
domestique a member of a professional cycling team, whose job is to ride solely for the benefit of the team and team leader, instead of their own glory
lanterne rouge the overall last-place rider in a stage race (from the red light found on the back of a train)

But as soon as things start going wrong, we're back to good old English:

bonk a cyclist's feeling of being devoid of energy
sag wagon the vehicle that carries bicyclists that have withdrawn from the event (due to injury, bicycle malfunction, tiredness etc.)

HEY DUDE!

Surfers follow the waves; and though you can find something to ride on in Newquay, they're altogether bigger, better and harder to stay on in Big Sur and Bondi . . .

shark biscuit (Australian slang *c.*1910) a novice surfer
hang five (US 1960s) to ride with the toes of one foot hooked over the front of the board
knots the bruises and cuts gained from battling the waves and his board (a surfer's status mark)
grubbing falling off your board while surfing
frube a surfer who does not catch a wave for the whole time they are in the water
hodad (1962) a show-off who hangs around surfing beaches, boasting of his exploits and trying to pick up girls, who has rarely, if ever, tried to surf
cowabunga! (Australian slang 1954) a shout of elation on surfing down a superb wave

COLORADO CLIFFHANGER

Climbing terms, likewise, come from mountainous places:

gingich (Scotland 1716) the chief climber or leader in climbing rocks
flash (Canada 1995) to climb a wall successfully on the first try
dynoing (Colorado 1992) leaping to a distant or out-of-reach hand hold
hang-dogging (Colorado 1992) a derogatory term for inexperienced climbers who hang on the rope while attempting feats beyond their ability

TROLLING AND YUMPING

Every sport, indeed, has both specialized terminology and also the kind of insiders' slang that makes seasoned practitioners feel quietly different, whether that be …

Rowing …

gully-shooting (b.1891) pointing oars upwards when rowing
gimp seat seat number 3 in an eight-person boat (often regarded as having the least responsibility)
blip-o! (late 19C) a derisive cry at a boat's coxswain colliding with anything

Tennis …

ketchepillar (early 16C) a tennis player
nacket (1833) a tennis ball-boy

Gymnastics …

coffee grinder a manoeuvre from a squatting position on the floor involving a circle of the leg while keeping both hands on the floor
fliffis a twisting double somersault performed on the trampoline
fly-away a horizontal-bar dismount method with a backward somersault

Billiards …

feather to run the cue backwards and forwards across the bridge between finger and thumb prior to making a shot
english the spin imparted to the ball
cocked hat a shot in which the ball hit by the white rebounds off three different cushions towards a middle pocket

or any of the other ways active people have found to pass their time, from long ago . . .

cock-squailing an old Shrove Tuesday sport involving flinging sticks at a cock tied by the leg, one penny per throw and whoever kills him takes him away

strag (Lancashire) to decoy other people's pigeons

trolling (Yorkshire) rolling hardboiled eggs down a slope (on Easter Monday)

dwile flunking (Suffolk) floorcloth throwing (a serious, competitive game)

postman's knock (Oxfordshire) a method of sliding on ice (by moving on one foot and tapping the ice with the other)

to right now . . .

to do an Ollie (skateboarding) to flip your ride in the air and stay aloft upon it

yump (rally-driving) to leave the ground in one's vehicle when going over a ridge

sandbagging (motorcycle racing) a stratagem whereby the favourite lets the rest of the field go on ahead, confident that when necessary he can regain the lead and win the race as expected

bulldogging (rodeo) to leap off a horse and then wrestle with a steer (the intention being to twist it by the horns and force it over onto the ground)

zorbing (New Zealand) harnessing oneself inside a huge inflatable PVC ball, then rolling more than 650 feet downhill

WORD JOURNEYS

upshot (16C) the final shot in archery that decided a match
racket (16C from Arabic via French) the palm of the hand
umpire (15C from Latin: *non par*, via Old French) not equal
gymnasium (16C from Ancient Greek via Latin) a school for exercising in the nude

RUBBY-DUBBY

Country pursuits

He that would have good luck in horses must kiss the parson's wife

(1678)

By long tradition in Britain, certain outdoor activities have been elevated to a higher category, that of 'field sports'. The most controversial of these is currently banned by law, though what this ban actually amounts to is anyone's guess:

own the moment in a hunt when the hounds show that they have found a scent

cut a voluntary to fall off one's horse while hunting

craner (*c.*1860) one who hesitates at a difficult jump

tantivy (1641) at full gallop

shoe-polisher a derisive term for a dog that doesn't stray far from a hunter's feet

TALLY HO!

Since 2004 deer can no longer be pursued with hounds in the UK, marking the end of a tradition dating back well before these terms from the Tudor–Stuart period:

abatures the traces left by a stag in the underwood through which he has passed
velvet-tip the down upon the first sprouting horns of a young deer
rascal a lean deer not fit to hunt
rechate the calling together of the hounds in hunting
dowcets the testicles of a deer

GAME ON

You may however still stalk and shoot these animals, as you may game birds such as pheasant or grouse. Which is perhaps ironic when you consider how much more efficient an instrument a gun is than a pack of hounds. As the Victorian dramatist W. S. Gilbert put it, 'Deer stalking would be a very fine sport if only the deer had guns'.

collimate (1837) to close an eye to aim at a target
nipshot (1568) in shooting: amiss in some way
fire into the brown (1871) shooting into the midst of a covey instead of singling out one bird
tailor (1889) to shoot at a bird, trying to miss
air washed a bird that lands and doesn't move or falls dead in the air and hits the ground (thus giving off very little scent on the ground and being difficult for dogs to find)
making game of a dog when it finds fresh scent

BIRDING

A gentler approach to our feathered friends has its own special terminology. And as any **birder** will tell you, it's simply not accurate to call them all **twitchers**:

squeaking noisily kissing the back of your hand in order to attract hidden birds
lifer a particular bird seen for the first time
getting a tick seeing a bird you've not seen before
gripping off seeing a bird when someone else doesn't
stringer a person suspected of lying about bird sightings
dipping out missing seeing a bird
whiffling of geese: descending rapidly from a height once the decision to land has been made, involving fast side-slipping first one way and then the other

GETTING HOOKED

Another ancient field sport remains highly unlikely to be banned (at least while Britain remains a democracy):

broggle (1653) to fish, especially for eels, by thrusting a sharp stick with bait on it into holes in the river bed
zulu (1898) an artificial fly
fizgig (1565) a kind of dart or harpoon with which seamen strike fish
guddle (1818) to catch trout by groping with the hands under the stones or banks of a stream
angletwitch (*c.*940) a worm used as bait in fishing
rubby-dubby (game fishing jargon) the minced fish (mackerel, pilchards etc.) used as a bait for larger fish especially sharks
angishore (Newfoundland) a man too lazy to fish

ROYAL FLUSH

One pursuit of folk from country and town alike is known also as 'the sport of kings', a moniker that certainly remains appropriate with our current crop of royals:

persuader (Australian slang) the jockey's whip
poppism (1653) the smacking sound with which riders encourage their horses
call a cab the jockey's action in waving one arm to hold his balance when he and the horse are taking a fence
drummer a horse that throws about his fore legs irregularly

morning glory a horse '**catching pigeons**' (showing great promise on the training gallops) but unable to repeat the form on a racetrack
airedale (US slang 1960s) a worthless racehorse
post the blue (b.1909) to win the Derby

GIFT HORSES

With large sums of money involved, the temptation to tamper with the proper result is as old as racing itself:

ingler (underworld slang 1797) a crooked horse breeder
bishop to disguise the age of a horse by tinkering with its teeth
drop anchor fraudulently to cause a horse to run slowly in a race
hook (New Zealand 1910) to ride a horse with the aim of losing

ODDS ON

Down by the track, there's little that passes the bookies by:

pencil-fever (*c.*1872) the laying of odds against a horse certain to lose
springer (UK slang 1922) a horse on which the odds suddenly shorten
skinner (Australian slang 1891) a horse which wins at long odds (a betting coup for bookmakers who do not have to pay out on a heavily backed favourite)
stickout (US slang 1937) a racehorse that seems a certain winner
nap (bookies' jargon) a racing tipster's best bet of the day
scaler (New Zealand 1908) a bookmaker who decamps without paying out

They've even developed their own method of communication without words, known as **tic-tac**, where they signal with their arms to communicate complicated changes in the odds to outside bookmakers. To these professionals, there's slang for any bet you care to make:

macaroni odds of 20/1
carpet odds of 3/1
elef a vier odds of 11/4
bottle odds of 2/1
shoulder odds of 7/4
ear'ole odds of 6/4
up the arm odds of 11/8
wrist odds of 5/4

VERY GOOD GOING

In the US and Australia (amongst other places) they have their own words for particular combinations of winners:

exacta or **perfecta** a wager in which the first two finishers in a race, in exact order of finish, must be picked
quinella a wager in which first two finishers must be picked, but payoff is made no matter which of the two wins and which runs second
trifecta to pick three horses in a particular race to finish 1st, 2nd and 3rd (the payout is determined by the betting pool on the turnover of the particular bet)
superfecta a bet that forecasts in correct order the first four horses in a given race

WORD JOURNEYS

jockeys (16C) horse traders (once called Jocks: men of the people)
allure (15C from Old French) to bait: a device in falconry used by hunters to call back their hawks
relay (15C from Old French) to loose the hounds; a pack of fresh hounds held in reserve to relieve a previous pack
croupier (18C from French) a pillion rider, a rider on the croup of a horse; then someone who stood behind a gambler and gave advice

MADHOUSE

Indoor games and hobbies

Cards and dice . . . the devil's books
and the devil's bones
(1676)

There's no shortage of enjoyable activities for those who would rather not brave our famously awful weather. Even the simplest-seeming have a complex terminology worth getting to know:

murgatroyd a badly manufactured tiddlywink, flat on both sides
squopped of a free tiddlywink that lands on another wink
blitz an attempt to pot all six winks of your own colour early in the game
crud a forceful shot whose purpose is to destroy a pile of winks completely
lunch to pot a squopped wink (usually belonging to an opponent)
boondock to send an opponent's tiddlywink a long way away, preferably off the table

LOW ROLLERS

The number of nicknames for marbles indicates what a popular game this is too (and still so in the age of the Game Boy® and the computer). In the dialect of the north-east of England, for example, marbles have been known as **alleys**, **boodies**, **glassies**, **liggies**, **marvels**, **muggles**, **penkers**, **parpers** and **scudders**. That's just the start of it:

flirt (Yorkshire) to flick a marble with finger and thumb

fullock (Shropshire) to shoot a marble in an irregular way by jerking the fist forward instead of hitting it off by the force of the thumb only

deegle (Cheshire) a stolen marble

neggy-lag (Yorkshire) the penultimate shot

hawk (Newfoundland) to win all an opponent's marbles

smuggings! (UK teen slang mid 19C) mine! (the exclamation used at the end of a game of marbles or spinning tops when the child who shouted first was allowed to keep the toy in question)

DICEMAN

When you get a little older, it becomes more interesting to throw objects with a more challenging set of possibilities:

snake eyes (North American slang 1929) getting double ones, the lowest score (supposedly resembling a snake's stare)

box cars (underworld slang 1937) double 6 (from their similarity to the wheels of freight cars)

gate to stop the dice moving before they have actually come to rest

ARRERS

Many grown-up indoor games are found in that fine old British institution, the pub. One pastime in particular speaks of generations of players with fine imaginations and plenty of time on their hands:

monger a person who deliberately scores many more points than needed to win the game

Robin Hood when a dart sticks into a previous dart

married man's side the left-hand side of a dart board (numbers 12, 9, 14, 11, 8 and 16) that would get a reasonable score (the rationale being a married man should always play safe)

right church, wrong pew hitting a double but the wrong number

slop darts that score, but not where you wanted them

masonry darts darts thrown so that they miss the board entirely and hit the wall instead

spray 'n' pray darts thrown by an irate and less talented player, rather quickly

bunting the art of throwing while on your knees

20 1 18 4 13 6 10 15 2 17 3 19 7 16 8 11 14 9 12 5

FEVVERS

And that's just a fraction of the jargon. All the scores in darts have their own names too. Remember, when playing darts you're counting down, not up, starting from a set 301 or 501 and trying to end up with exactly zero, a process which is known as **doubling out**:

madhouse double 1 (i.e. what you're left in until you finish the game by achieving it)
fevvers a score of 33 (from the 19C Cockney tongue twister: 'thirty-three feathers on a thrush's throat')
scroat a dart that is aimed for treble 20, but ends up in double 20
fish and globe a score of 45 (when competing on a fairground darts stall, 45 was a score that traditionally would win the customer a small paper bag of peanuts which later became the offer of a jar (globe) and a goldfish)
Lord Nelson a score of 111 (as he had one eye, one arm, one leg)

POKER FACE

A cool head and an expressionless face will serve you well in a game that otherwise relies on luck – unless of course you have other tricks up your sleeve:

runt a poker hand worth less than a pair
motown a poker hand consisting of 'jacks-on-fives'
vole the winning by one player of all the tricks of a deal; a grand-slam
pone the player who cuts the cards
hop a secret move made after the cut which puts the cards back in the original position and negates that cut for the cheat's benefit
crimp to bend one or more cards so that a cheat will be able to cut the deck as he wishes, or to know that an innocent player will be cutting the deck at that same desired card
there's work down the announcement by one player that someone somehow is cheating

BIDDING WAR

The king of card games requires not just luck, but skill of the highest level:

chicane (1886) the condition in a game of bridge of holding no trumps
bumble-puppy (1936) a game played at random (of people who play no conventions)
yarborough (19C) a bridge or whist hand with no card higher than a 9 (from a certain Earl of Yarborough who used to bet 1000 to 1 against the occurrence of such a hand; the actual odds are 1827 to 1)
flag-flying (1917) to make an overbid that will almost inevitably fail, just to liven up the game
huddle (US 1934) a period of thought in which a player considers his next move

FULL HOUSE

For those habitués of the pack, there's a fine range of nicknames for individual cards:

devil's bed-post (*c.*1835) the four of clubs, held to be unlucky
grace-card (Irish mid 19C) the six of hearts in cards
curse of Scotland (early 18C) the nine of diamonds (diamonds imply royalty and traditionally every ninth king of Scotland has been considered a tyrant and a curse to that country)
blankets (1915) the tens in a pack of cards (from the rolling of blankets in the military in tens for the convenience of transport)
noddy (Gloucestershire) the knave
suicide king the king of hearts (as the fifteenth-century French picture shows him about to impale himself on his sword)
the boy with the boots (Anglo-Irish late 19C) the joker in the pack of cards

HIGH STAKES

When you start to bring money into the picture, of course, both dice and cards can easily lose their innocence:

shill a decoy player, allied to the promoters of the game, who pretends to bet, and is allowed to 'win' in street games of three-card monte; his successes are intended to lure the public into laying down their money
tattogey (underworld slang 1753) one who uses loaded dice to cheat
langret (mid 16C) a die so loaded that it shows 3 or 4 more often than any other number

DESPERATE BIDS

For some unfortunates, the impulse to win can stop being a game and become more a part of their lives. As the Aussies say, there are some people who would **bet on two flies walking up the wall**:

martingale to continue doubling one's stake after losing in the hope of eventual recovery

ring in one's nose to be losing and betting heavily and impetuously in an attempt to get even (like a bull)

fishing remaining in a card game in the hope of a vital card

bird dog a small time or novice gambler who hangs around experienced professional gamblers to pick up tips

nut the living expenses and other overheads that a gambler must meet from his winnings

MONTE CARLO OR BUST

For people like this, home games are soon no longer enough; a professional arena for their habit beckons; and there, of course, under the patina of respectability, pretty much anything goes:

ladder man a casino employee who sits on a high chair and watches for any errors or cheating by players or croupiers

booster a bit player in a casino who entices genuine players to bet (and usually lose) their money

top-hatting in roulette, the surreptitious placing of more casino chips on top of existing ones after the outcome has been decided

BINGO LINGO

Better to switch to a sociable game often favoured by the older woman, which comes with its own inimitable terminology. **Two fat ladies** (88) and **legs eleven** are well-known but there are many other traditional coinages:

1 buttered scone
6 Tom Mix (more modern: **chopsticks**)
7 Gawd's in 'eaven
12 monkey's cousin (from rhyming slang for dozen)
23 a duck and a flea (from the shape of the figures)
50 half-way house (1940s) (since there are 100 numbers available to the caller)
76 was she worf it? (from 7/6d, the old price of a marriage licence)
77 two little crutches (from the shape of the figures)
80 Gandhi's breakfast (as he 'ate nothing')

ANORAKS

Or else give it up entirely and settle on a worthwhile and productive hobby:

notaphily (1970) the collecting of paper currency as a hobby
deltiologist (1959) a collector of picture postcards
cartophily (1936) the hobby of collecting cigarette cards
arctophile (1970s) a person who loves or collects teddy bears
cruciverbalist (US slang 1970s) a crossword puzzle addict
bowerbird (Australian slang) a person who collects an astonishing array of sometimes useless objects

notaphily
cruciverbalist
deltiologist
cartophily
ladder mesh
bird dog
cartophile
booster
top hatting

WORD JOURNEYS

hazard (13C) a game of dice
forfeit (13C from Latin via Old French) 'done beyond the bounds of' the law, a crime
depart (13C from Latin via Old French) to divide into parts, distribute

MUSH FAKERS AND APPLESQUIRES

The world of work

He that hopes to thrive must rise at five;
he that has thriven, may lie till seven;
but he that will never thrive
may lie till eleven

(1640)

Even in these days of welfare, or **national handbag** as Polari slang (see page 157) evocatively has it, most of us have to work at something to make ends meet. However specialized or odd our occupation may be, we can take comfort from the fact that in harsher times, jobs came in all shapes and sizes:

legger (Yorkshire) a man employed to move canal boats through tunnels by walking on the roof or sides of the tunnel
fottie (Scottish) a female wool-gatherer
murenger (Cheshire 1706) an officer appointed to keep the walls of a city in repair
sewer (Tudor–Stuart) an attendant at a meal who superintended the seating of the guests and the tasting and the serving of the dishes
shore-man (Cockney) one who searches sewers for rats
pure-finder (*c.*1850) a street collector of dogs' dung
applesquire (late 16C) the male servant of a prostitute

gong-farmer (1596) a person who cleaned out privies at night and sold the waste as a fertilizer

screever (1851) a professional writer of begging letters

glutman (1796) a temporary customs officer hired because of his ability to be numerate

lodger-remover (underworld slang 1889) a seller of fine-toothed haircombs

mush faker (1821) an umbrella repairer ('mushroom-faker')

resurrection doctor (1800s) a doctor who buys corpses which are stolen from graves, or has people murdered and delivered to him

whiffler (1539) an officer armed with a weapon who clears the way for a procession

COLOUR CODED

Nowadays many jobs can be seen as either **white** or **blue collar**, where the former are those who wear a suit and work in offices, and the latter those getting their hands dirty in a boilersuit. The designation white came first, in 1921, and blue followed in 1950. Since then imaginative business writers and others have added yet more categories:

pink (1975) secretaries and other clerical staff

steel (1980) robots

grey (1981) skilled technicians; employees whose job descriptions combine some white- and some blue-collar duties

green (1984) environmentalists

gold (1985) professionals or those with in-demand skills; employees over 55

black (1998) miners (especially coal miners) and oil workers

scarlet (2000) female pornographic shop operators

ELBOW GREASE

But whatever your job, whether it be typing at a word-processor or hauling coal, there is one element in common: at some point you have to get stuck in to doing the work:

swallow the frog to tackle the hardest task possible
knife-and-fork it to deal with it bit by bit
antisocordist (1680) an opponent of laziness or idiocy
fluttergrub (Sussex) a man who takes a delight in working about in the dirt, and getting into every possible mess
work for Jesus (US industrial relations) to put in extra work without asking for extra pay

JOBSWORTH

Of course there are always those who manage to slow productivity in some way or other. As the Australians say, they're **as useless as an ashtray on a motorbike**:

chair plug (2006) someone who sits in a meeting but contributes nothing
boondoggle (1935) to carry out valueless or extremely trivial work in order to convey the impression that one is busy
to be on the shockell (Warwickshire) to neglect one's work through beer
headless nail (1950s) a worker who, once he got into a job, was impossible to get out, even if unsuitable
sunlighting (US 1980s) doing a quite different job on one day of the working week

BRAINSTORMING

Ideas, as they say, are two a penny. But a sudden brainwave can be worth a month of pointless toil:

quaesitum (1748) the answer to a problem
just-add-water (UK current office jargon) an idea that is so brilliantly simple yet effective that it requires little by way of preparation
limbeck (1599) to rack or fatigue the brain in an effort to have a new idea

NO-DAY

However hard we try not to, we all have those days where our hard work seems to come to nought:

blue duck (New Zealand 1890) something unprofitable
windmill-tilt (US jargon 2006) a fruitless and frustrating venture: attacking imaginary enemies or fighting otherwise-unwinnable battles
salmon day (1990s) the entire day spent swimming upstream only to get screwed in the end

PUSHING THE ENVELOPE

The jargon of contemporary corporate life may seem absurd to the outsider, rich as it is in the most colourful of metaphors. But it's certainly guaranteed to brighten up even the dullest day:

takeaway nuggets insights or information resulting from a meeting or interaction

sunset clauses stipulations that a contract or regulation will lapse unless renewed

to wash its own face to justify or pay for itself

push the peanut to progress an arduous and delicate task forward

ketchup-bottle a long period of inertia followed by a burst of exaggerated activity; the unplanned release of pent-up forces

swallow your own smoke to take responsibility for and/or suffer the consequences of your mistakes

MANAGERIE

Why are things so often discussed in animal terms? Is it because of a desperate subliminal desire to get out of the office?

shoot the puppy to dare to do the unthinkable
prairie dogging popping one's head above an office cubicle out of curiosity or to spy on colleagues
lipstick on a pig an attempt to put a favourite spin on a negative situation
a pig in a python a surge in a statistic measured over time
boiling frog syndrome a company which fails to recognize gradual market change (as a slowly boiled frog may not detect a slow temperature increase)
moose on the table an issue which everyone in a business meeting knows is a problem but which no one wants to address
seagull manager a manager who flies in, makes a lot of noise, shits all over everything, and then leaves

THANK GOD IT'S FRIDAY – OFFICE ACRONYMS

SWOT Strengths, Weaknesses, Opportunities, Threats (a favourite of consultants)
PICNIC Problem In Chair, Not In Computer
WOMBAT Waste Of Money, Brains And Time
POET'S day Piss Off Early Tomorrow's Saturday (refers to Friday)

BULLS AND BEARS

In good times and bad, the highly paid practitioners of both the City of London and Wall Street have couched their dubious activities in their own specialized jargon:

J-Lo (Wall Street) the rounding bottom in a stock's price chart (after the curvaceous Jennifer Lopez)

Bo Derek (Wall Street) the perfect stock (after her famous film *10*)

poop and scoop to drive down a share price by spreading malicious rumours

mattressing the term used by other traders and bank managers to hide their results

barefoot pilgrim someone who has lost everything on the stock market, but might still be persuaded to invest again

catch a falling knife to buy a stock as its price is going down, in the hope that it will go back up, only to have it continue to fall

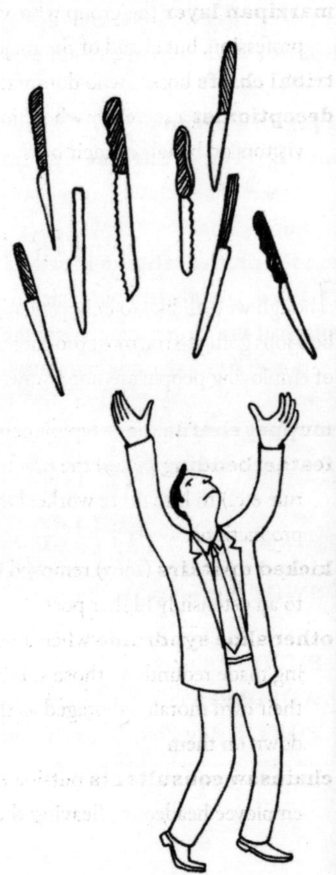

ROOM AT THE TOP

If you have ability, however, and enough patience to continue to play the game, you will slowly but surely make your way up the corporate ladder:

royal jelly flashy projects fed to someone whom the boss is grooming for promotion
marzipan layer the group who are ranked below the very top in their profession, but ahead of the majority
tribal chiefs bosses who dominate through charisma and patronage
deceptionist a secretary whose job it is to delay or block potential visitors on behalf of their boss

FIRM HAND

Though we'd all like to believe that hard work is always rewarded, with the best jobs going to the most productive people, the sad fact is that the realities of employing people are not always so straightforward:

muppet shuffle the redeployment of problem staff
featherbedding (1949) the practice of forcing the employer (by union rule etc.) to hire more workers than needed (or to limit his workers' production)
kicked upstairs (1967) removed from the scene of action by promotion to an ostensibly higher post
other shoe syndrome when a number of executives in a firm are being made redundant, those survivors, rather than feeling relieved, find their own morale sabotaged as they wait for 'the other shoe' to come down on them
chainsaw consultants outside experts brought in to reduce the employee headcount (leaving the top brass with clean hands)

THE SACK

So unpleasant is it to ask people to clear their desks and take their skills elsewhere, that a huge number of words and phrases has grown up to euphemistically describe the simple fact of redundancy. You might have been **handed your cards** or perhaps you're **clearing your desk, considering your position** or maybe becoming a **consultant**. Maybe you've been **deselected** or you're taking an **early bath**. Then again, perhaps you're **excess to requirements** or you've even been **excluded**. You're leaving to **give time to your other commitments** or else you're off on **gardening leave**. If you're lucky you'll have negotiated a **golden handshake** rather than merely being given a **leave of absence** or **let go**. When you're **given notice** let's hope they don't say it's **natural wastage** or that you've been **stood down**. No, you're **spending more time with your wife and family**, as it's your right to do, even if your **contract has been terminated** and nobody could really describe this as a **voluntary relocation**.

SMALL IS BETTER

As for the ruthless companies themselves, why, they're doing nothing more unnatural than a bit of **decruitment**. They are in fact **degrowing**, **dehiring**, **delayering** and **destaffing**. In a process of **downsizing** some employees have had to take **early release**. Yes, there is a bit of **executive outplacement** and **force reduction** going on. Shall we call it **internal reorganization**? Nobody is being **put out to grass**. There's been a **personnel surplus reduction**, indeed a straightforward **rationalization of the workforce**. Some people have been **redeployed**. There's been a bit of **restructuring**, some **retrenching** and **rightsizing**, not to mention **schedule adjustment**, **selective separation** and **skill-mix adjustment**. It's all nothing more than a bit of **transitioning**, **vocational relocation** and **workforce imbalance correction**.

MY OLD MAN'S A . . .

Once upon a time, we were all quite happy to say exactly what it was we did. But as status has become ever more important, some quite straightforward occupations have developed some quite preposterous titles:

vision clearance engineer a window cleaner
stock replenishment adviser a shelf stacker
dispatch services facilitator a post room worker
head of verbal communications a receptionist/secretary
environment improvement technician a cleaner

HAWKERS AND HUCKSTERS

However you dress him (or her) up, there's no denying that a salesman is always a salesman. It's an occupation that's been around since men first started trading beads and barley:

chafferer (1382) a vendor who enjoys talking while making a sale
mangonize (Tudor–Stuart) to sell men or boys for slaves
bend-down plaza (Jamaican English) a row of roadside pedlars, specializing in items that are hard to get in shops, because of import restrictions
amster (Australian slang 1941) one who works outside a carnival, sideshow, strip club etc. touting the pleasures inside and pulling in the customers
click (1748) to stand at a shop-door and invite customers in
jaw-work! (mid 18C) a cry used in fairs by the sellers of nuts

WIDOWS AND ORPHANS

These guys know the price of everything, and its value too, and they've plenty of lingo to describe what they're trying to get rid of...

zhing-zhong (Zimbabwean slang) merchandise made in Asia; cheaply made, inexpensive or substandard goods
halo model a super-product which enhances an entire brand
orphan (second-hand motor trade jargon) any discontinued model of a car
widow's piano inferior instruments sold as bargains (from an advertisement announcing that a widow lady is compelled to sell her piano, for which she will take half price)

...how they do it...

deaconing (US slang 1866) the practice of packing food so that the finest specimens are visible
shillaber (North American slang 1913) someone posing as an enthusiastic or successful customer to encourage other buyers
trotting (auction jargon) the tactic whereby a dealer's ring will force an outsider up to an unrealistically high bid, at which point they will drop out and leave their rival with a large bill
bovrilise (1901) to condense an advertisement to essentials

...and those to whom they're pitching their spiel...

nose picker a salesman's derogatory description of a potential client who cannot make up their mind and has no power of decision-making within the firm
twack (Newfoundland 1937) a shopper who looks at goods, inquires about prices but buys nothing
grey panthers (US slang) assertive and/or exigent elderly consumers

THE READIES

At the end of it there's one glorious commodity that makes it all worthwhile:

stadge (Lancashire and Cheshire) the date of issue stamped upon coins
mule (industry jargon) a coin or note which has two mismatched sides
drink-link (UK students' slang 2000) a cash dispenser
squiddish (Northumberland) the twentieth part of a farthing
chapmoney (Shropshire) money which the seller gives back to the buyer for luck
wergeld (1214) money paid by the killer's family by way of compensation to free the offender from further punishment
fornale (1478) to spend one's money before it has been earned

LILIES OF THE FIELD

Although for some fortunate people, such vulgar considerations really don't figure:

oofy (1896) rich
slippage (US slang 2005) the percentage of people who get a cheque and forget to cash it
set the Thames on fire (UK late 18C) to make a great success in life
stalko (1802) a man who has nothing to do and no fortune to support him but who styles himself as a squire

WORD JOURNEYS

robot (20C from Czech) servitude, forced labour
cattle (13C) property, wealth; then (16C) moveable property; then livestock
up the spout (UK slang b1894) from the spout (lift) used in pawnbrokers' shops; when items were handed over in return for money they were sent 'up the spout' to the storeroom where they stayed until their owner could afford to redeem them
customer (14C) a customs house officer; then (16C) someone the customs officer had to deal with

BULK AND FILE

Crime and punishment

He that helpeth an evill man,
hurteth him that is good

(1597)

The line between making money by sheer hard work and from more dubious practices has always been thin:

vigerage (underworld slang 1935) a loan shark's 20 per cent weekly interest

flim-flam (underworld slang 1881) the various dodges by which a thief, in changing money, obtains more than he gives from tradesmen and bank-tellers

mocteroof (costermongers' jargon 1860) to doctor damaged fruit or vegetables

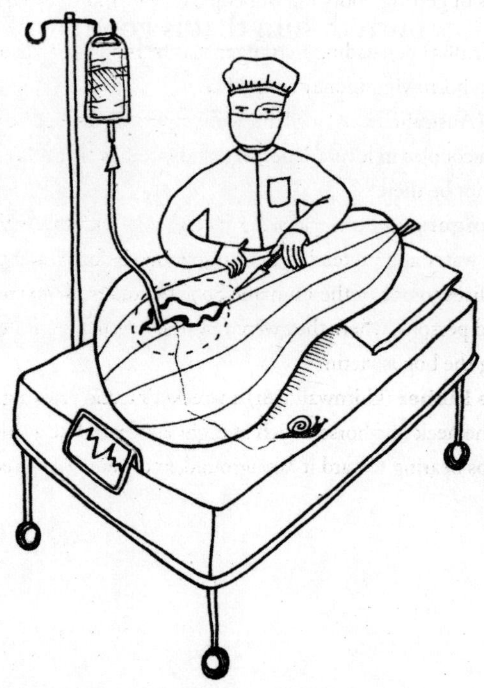

striping the lot (North American slang) the painting of the parking lot at a new shopping mall with extra-wide spacing for the positioning of cars (this gives the impression of the mall attracting more customers than it really does, and when business picks up, the spaces can be repainted somewhat narrower)

quomodocunquize (1652) to make money by any means possible

MY DEAR FELLOW!

Other ways of getting booty out of people may be more extreme:

gagging (*c.*1825) persuading a stranger that he is an old acquaintance and then borrowing money from him

bull trap (Australia 1930s) a villain who impersonates a policeman and preys on couples in lovers' lanes, extorting money from those who should not be there

queer plungers (underworld slang 1785) crooks who threw themselves into the water and pretended to be drowning, before being taken by accomplices to one of the Humane Society houses for the recovery of drowned persons, where they were rewarded with a guinea each for rescuing the bogus victim

jibber the kibber (Cornwall 1781) a wrecker's tactic of fixing a lantern round the neck of a horse which at night appeared like a ship's light. The ships bearing toward it ran aground, and were plundered by the locals

NOT QUITE MY COLOUR

Even the most upright of us may not be totally straight all the time:

wardrobing (US slang) buying an item and then returning it after wearing it
bilker (1717) a person who gives a cabman less than his fare and, when remonstrated with, gives a false name and address
manoeuvring the apostles (b.1811) robbing Peter to pay Paul (i.e. borrowing from one man to pay another)
oyster (underworld slang 1920) a society woman employed to wear stolen jewellery in the hope that she will receive an offer from a fence, and will, because of her social position, remain unsuspected by the police

PANHANDLER

Just because you've been reduced to begging, it doesn't mean that you're dishonest. Having said that, some bums have always known that cheating pays:

dommerers (1567) men who pretended to be deaf and dumb
cleymes (b.1811) artificial sores, made by beggars to excite charity
scaldrum dodge (mid 19C) the practice of deliberately burning the body with a mixture of acids and gunpowder to simulate scars and wounds to soften the hearts of those from whom one begs
whip-jacks (1562) vagabonds who pretended to be shipwrecked sailors
aurium (16C) a wandering beggar posing as some kind of priest

CUTPURSE

Others, fitter and more fleet of foot, make better boodle by being proactive:

maltooling (b.1861) the picking of pockets in omnibuses
bulk and file (1698) two pickpockets operating together (the **bulk** jostles the party that is to be robbed and the **file** steals the treasure)
reef (*c*.1860) to draw up a dress-pocket until a purse is within reach of the fingers
pappy (underworld slang 1910) an elderly man whose clothes and pockets are baggy (the ideal victim for a pickpocket)

SLEIGHT OF HAND

As in many another career paths, the professional pilferer, too, likes to develop his expert knowledge:

feeder-prigger (late 18C) a thief specializing in silver spoons
badger (US mid 19C) a rogue who specializes in robbing clients who are visiting a brothel
efter (underworld slang 1846) a thief who robs theatre patrons during a show
tinny-hunter (late 18C) a thief who robs people whose homes are burning down, while pretending to give assistance
vamper (mid 19C) a thief who deliberately starts fights between others in order to rob them in the confusion
tosher (b.1859) one who steals copper from the bottom of ships moored in the Thames

ARTFUL DODGERS

Other tricks of the trade definitely make a crook's life easier and more productive:

trigging the jigger (early 19C) placing a small piece of paper (**trig**) in the front door keyhole of a house that is presumed to be uninhabited; if the paper is still there a day later, the robber can believe that the house is empty and can be broken into safely

treacle-man (late 19C) a good-looking man who works as a decoy for burglars by charming the housemaid while the gang slip in unnoticed

snudge (underworld slang 1665) a thief who hides himself under a bed in order to rob the house

little snakesman (1781) a little boy who gets into a house through the sink-hole, and then opens the door for his accomplices

DOLPHINS AND TURTLES

Underworld slang, old and new, covers a whole range of dodgy activity, from the relatively harmless to the downright evil:

shoulder surf (UK current slang) to use a pair of binoculars to read the PIN of people using cash dispensers

slaughter (1950s) an immediate dumping ground for recently stolen property, before it is shared out or hidden more permanently and securely

turn turtle (early 19C) to flip a carriage upside-down

airmail (US prison jargon 1950s) concrete, bricks and so on hurled down from rooftops onto patrol cars responding to a call

rifling (underworld slang 1885) plundering dead bodies in the river (especially the Thames) and turning them adrift again

make one's bones (New York slang 1969) to kill a person as a requirement for membership in a criminal gang

OLD BILL

One gang who know more about all this than most are society's upholders of the law, who have a few tricks of their own up their sleeves:

flash roll (police jargon) a wad of money which is never actually used, but is flashed ostentatiously around to convince a criminal, e.g. a drug dealer, that one wishes to make a purchase, at which point an arrest will be made

Kojak with a Kodak (US 1970s) a policeman manning a radar speed trap

mule kick (US slang 2005) the act of standing with one's back to the front door and kicking the door in

attitude-adjuster (US black slang) a club; a police officer's stick

to get a fanner (Hobo slang) to be hit on the soles while sleeping on a park bench and moved on by the police

ghetto bird (US slang) a police helicopter

wiggle seat (US police jargon) a special lie detector that can be fitted to a chair and which will measure the bodily reactions of a suspect to various crucial questions

BAD APPLES

Upstanding members of society can only hope that their local rozzers are worthy of the power entrusted in them:

mumping (UK slang 1970) the acceptance by the police of small gifts or bribes from tradespeople

swim in golden grease (UK slang 17C) to receive many bribes

banana (UK street slang 1990s) a corrupt police officer (initially of the Special Patrol Group because they were, allegedly, yellow, bent and hanging around in bunches)

shoo-fly (US slang 1877) a policeman, usually in plain clothes, whose job is to watch and report on other police officers

accommodation collar (US police jargon) an arrest only made to raise the officer's arrest record and thus improve his standing in the hierarchy

JUST DESERTS

There are some who would prefer that criminals were treated with the summary justice of yesteryear; without faffing around with all that tedious business of innocent until proved guilty:

alfet (*c.*1000) a vat of boiling water into which the accused plunged his arm in lieu of a trial

keelhaul (1626) to punish in the seamen's way, by dragging the criminal under water on one side of the ship and up again on the other

ride the stang (UK b.1828) to be carried on a pole through the town on men's shoulders and pelted with refuse for the amusement of a hooting crowd (a derisive punishment for a breach of decorum or morality, especially on the part of a married man)

corsned (Anglo-Saxon law *c.*1000) a trial by ordeal that required a suspect to eat a piece of barley bread and cheese to test his innocence (if guilty, it was believed the bread would cause convulsions and choking)

whiffler (underworld slang 1859) a fellow who cries out in pain

PETTIFOGGERS

Undoubtedly the intervention of the legal profession does complicate matters, and sometimes completely unnecessarily:

kilburn (police jargon) the official police notebook that is produced in court (rhyming slang: Kilburn Priory for diary)

gunner (US slang 2004) a law student who always needs to volunteer an answer to show off how smart they are

ambulance-chaser (underworld slang 1897) a lawyer who attends scenes of accidents and hospitals to get business from the injured or bereaved, who are not in a position to resist

dock asthma (police and prison jargon 1950s) gasps of (usually feigned) surprise and disbelief by prisoners in the dock

boot-eater (1880) a juror who would rather 'eat his boots' than find a person guilty

PORRIDGE

A spell inside should be enough to make anyone think twice about reoffending:

oubliette (Scott: *Ivanhoe* 1819) a dungeon whose only entrance is in the ceiling
dry bath (1933) a search of a prisoner who has been stripped naked
broken arse (New Zealand) a prisoner who has sided with the authorities and thus ranked the lowest in the inmate hierarchy
carpy (1940s) locked away in one's cell at night (from Latin tag *carpe diem* for 'seize the day')
to polish the King's iron with one's eyebrows (underworld slang 1785) to look longingly out of prison windows

Although not necessarily so:

gate fever (UK slang 2007) terror at the prospect of release from prison
phoenix (underworld slang 1925) one who enters the world after long imprisonment
boomerang (US slang) to return to prison almost immediately on finishing the last sentence

CLEAN SHIRT

Career criminals have always had to make calculations about the possible punishment they may have to endure, leading to a wide range of names for different prison sentences. Here's a selection:

thirteen clean shirts (late 19C) three months' imprisonment (at the rate of one shirt a week)
magazine (US 1920s) a six month jail sentence (the time it would take to read one if one could barely read)
the clock (Australian slang 1950) twelve months' imprisonment (from the hours on a clock face)
pontoon (UK prison jargon 1950) a twenty-one month jail sentence (from the card-game in which a score of twenty-one is the optimum hand)
rouf (UK back slang* 1851) a four year sentence
taxi (US slang 1930) between five and fifteen years' imprisonment (from the fares in cents displayed in New York taxis)
neves (UK back slang* 1901) a seven year sentence
work under the armpits (early 19C) to confine one's criminality to such activities that would be classed as petty larceny (bringing a maximum sentence of seven years' transportation rather than hanging)
working above the armpits (early 19C) to commit crimes that could lead to one's execution

* Slang that works when read or written backwards

WORD JOURNEYS

to pay on the nail (1596) from a practice in medieval markets where instant justice was dealt to those who reneged on agreements or cheated their customers. Eventually it was decided that accounts be settled at counters (short pillars known as nails) in the open market place and in front of witnesses. Payments were placed on these counters for everyone to see that all was correct

not enough room to swing a cat (1771) refers to the whip used on board ships for dealing out punishment (the whip started as a cat-of-three-tails but became a cat-of-nine-tails by the end of the seventeenth century; this method of punishment continued until 1875)

nipper (16C) a thief, person who nipped or pinched; then (19C) a costermonger's boy attendant

villain (14C from Latin via Old French) a worker on a country estate (in feudal terms the lord was the great landowner, and under him were a host of tenants called villains; the notion of wickedness and worthlessness is simply the effect of aristocratic pride and exclusivity)

BUNTING TIME

Matters of love

After your fling,
watch for the sting

(1917)

The beginning of love is often physical. In hiphop male attractiveness is described as **pimp-juice** and its female counterpart as **milkshake**, contemporary versions of a long tradition:

bobbant (Wiltshire) of a girl: forward, romping
featous (mid 14C) of a man: handsome, good looking
clipsome (1816) eminently embraceable

DISCO JUDGES

Women have long known just how critical others can be of their looks, whether they be English country folk or American teenagers:

sinful-ordinary (Wiltshire) plain to the last degree in looks
bridlegged (Cheshire) a farmer's contemptuous description of a woman as having legs not strong enough to work on the farm
sphinx (US black teen slang) a woman who is beautiful from the neck up
Medusa (US black teen slang) a woman who is beautiful from the neck down
strobe-light honey (US black teen slang) a woman who seems attractive in flickering light but not otherwise

ZEPPELINS

One aspect in particular often receives close attention:

bathycolpian (1825) having a deep cleavage
headlamps (UK slang early 20C) female breasts: this was when large, raised car headlights were the norm (a century earlier the common expression was **barges**)
dead heat in a Zeppelin race (UK slang) an admiring description of large breasts
fore-buttocks (Pope: *The Dunciad* 1727) breasts
Cupid's kettledrums (18C) breasts

SUPERSIZE ME

So how do you get your feelings across? **Do fries go with that shake**? was a phrase called out by black men in 1970s America to a passing woman they fancied; while the object of admiration might mutter to her friend: **He can put his shoes under my bed anytime** . . .

boombaloomba (Australian slang) an expression of a man's attraction to a woman
look that needs suspenders (1940s) a very interested glance at a woman (the suspenders were needed to keep the man's eyeballs attached to their sockets)

HUNTER DITHERERS

Not that everyone finds it easy to be so forward:

stick-up (Wiltshire) to make the first tentative advances towards courting
dangle (late 18C) to follow a woman without actually addressing her
quirkyalone (US slang 1999) someone who just wants the right person to come along at the right time even if that means waiting

FAINT HEART

Sometimes one just has to take the risk and get a bit proactive:

tapper (1950s) a boy who repeatedly pestered a girl for a date
wingwoman (US slang from the film *Top Gun* 1986) a professional female matchmaker who escorts a man to a bar or club, engages in light conversation to draw in other females, and then withdraws
strike breaker (1920s) a young woman who was ready to date her friend's beau when a couple's romance was coming to an end
rabbit's-kiss (Anglo-Manx) a penalty in the game of 'forfeits' in which a man and woman have each to nibble the same piece of straw until their lips meet

DELIGHTFUL

Until 1958 debutantes and their mothers exchanged information about the respectable young men to whom they were introduced by using a special code:

FU Financially Unsound
MTF Must Touch Flesh
MSC Makes Skin Crawl
NSIT Not Safe In Taxis
VVSITPQ Very, Very Safe In Taxis, Probably Queer

THE WILDER SHORES OF LOVE

As homosexuality was illegal in the UK until 1967, the secret language of Polari was used to disguise gay subculture from the disapproving gaze of the law. It was originally used by circus and fairground performers who were equally keen to communicate with each other without their audience understanding. Drawn from Italian, Yiddish, Cockney rhyming slang and full of backwards words (such as **ecaf** for face) Polari provided various terms that we all use today, such as **drag**, **camp** and **bimbo,** as well as some less well-known but equally colourful expressions:

omi-polone a gay man (literally man-woman; a lesbian was **polone-omi**, a woman-man)
alamo hot for him
basket the bulge of male genitals through trousers
naff awful, dull, bad (said to stand for Not Available For F***ing)

CHEAP DATE

Whatever your proclivities, there are numerous reasons why one should beware of giving too much too soon:

couch cootie (US 1920s) a poor or miserly man who prefers to court a woman in her own house than take her out on the town
flat-wheeler (US college slang 1920s) a young man whose idea of entertaining a girl is to take her for a walk
cream-pot love (b.1811) professed by insincere young men to dairy-maids, to get cream and other goods from them

GETTING DOWN TO IT

In the less permissive 1950s, a **Nottingham goodnight** was the phrase used of a courting couple who had got back from their date, and then slammed the door and said 'goodnight' loudly before retiring quietly to the sofa, hoping they would not be disturbed for some time . . .

suaviation (1656) a love kiss
cow-kissing (US slang mid 19C) kissing with much movement of the tongues and lips
lallygagger (1920s) a courting male who liked to kiss his sweetheart in hallways
bundling (b.1811) a man and a woman sleeping in the same bed, he with his clothes on, and she with her petticoat on

COUNTRY LOVING

But if the weather's good, why bother to go home at all?

sproag (Scotland late 16C) to run among the haystacks after the girls at night

to give a girl a green gown (late 16C) to tumble her onto the grass

bunting time (1699) when the grass is high enough to hide young men and maids courting

boondock (Tennessee campus slang b.1950) to neck, pet or make love in an automobile

gulch (Newfoundland 1895) to frequent a sheltered hollow to engage in sexual intimacy

SEALED WITH A LOVING KISS – LOVE LETTER ACRONYMS

During the Second World War all mail was opened and read by the official Censor. So acronyms of places written on the backs of envelopes were used to convey secret messages of love (and lust) between servicemen and their wives or girlfriends:

HOLLAND Hope Our Love Lasts And Never Dies
MEXICO CITY May Every Kiss I Can Offer Carry Itself To You
MALAYA My Ardent Lips Await Your Arrival
CHINA Come Home I Need Affection
NORWICH (K)nickers Off Ready When I Come Home
BURMA Be Undressed Ready My Angel
EGYPT Eager to Grab Your Pretty Tits
SIAM Sexual Intercourse At Midnight

ALL LOVED UP

Limerence (US Connecticut 1977) is the word for that initial exhilarating rush of falling in love, the state of 'being in love'. During that time the besotted of either sex should be careful not to **deff out**, the American slang for women who immediately lose contact with their female friends after acquiring a steady boyfriend. And this is just one of the pitfalls of sudden love:

fribbler (1712) one who professes rapture for a woman, but dreads her consent

batmobiling (US slang) putting up protective emotional shields just as a relationship enters an intimate, vulnerable stage (with reference to the car's retracting armour)

THEY FLEE FROM ME

Once things start to go wrong, the slide can be all too rapid . . .

to wear the willow (late 16C) to have been abandoned by one's lover

. . . so do try and avoid being cynical . . .

sorbet sex (US slang popularized by *Sex and the City*) a casual sexual relationship undertaken in the period between two more serious relationships

pull a train (US slang 1965) sexual intercourse with a succession of partners (like a string of boxcars, they have to be coupled and uncoupled)

... or sentimental ...

desiderium (Swift: letter to Pope 1715) a yearning for a thing one once had but has lost

anacampserote (1611) a herb that can bring back departed love

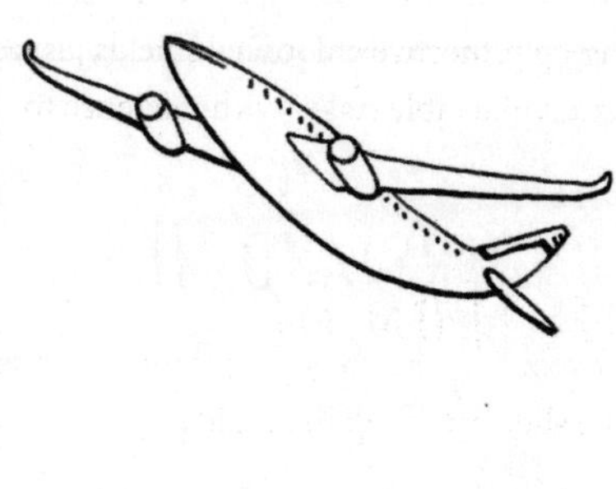

DROIT DE SEIGNEUR

Take heart from the fact that anything goes; and the history of love tells of some decidedly odd arrangements:

gugusse (early 1880s) an effeminate youth who frequents the private company of priests
panmixis (1889) a population in which random mating takes place
Shunamitism (b.1901) the practice of an old man sleeping with, but not necessarily having sex with, a young woman to preserve his youth (the rationale was that the heat of the young woman would transfer to the old man and revitalize him, based on the Biblical story of King David and Abishag)

HE DOESN'T UNDERSTAND ME

Just beware the types for whom lovemaking has become habitual (or even professional):

mud-honey (Tennyson: *Maud* 1855) the dirty pleasures of men about town
cougar (Canadian slang 2005) an older woman on the prowl, preferably for a younger man
lovertine (1603) someone addicted to sex
play checkers (US gay jargon 1960s) to move from seat to seat in a cinema in search of a receptive sex partner
twopenny upright (UK slang 1958) the charge made by a prostitute for an act of sexual intercourse standing up out of doors

WORD JOURNEYS

boudoir (French 18C) a place to sulk or pout in
friend (Old English) a lover; then (12C) a relative or kinsman
buxom (12C) obedient, compliant; then (16C) plump and comely
harem (17C from Turkish via Arabic) forbidden to others; then sacred to the women and their apartments

WITTOLS AND BEER BABIES

Marriage and family life

Marriage halves our griefs,
doubles our joys,
and quadruples our expenses

(1902–4)

However giddy and capricious at first, it's certainly true that Love moves, inexorably, towards the recognized and the formalized:

wooer-bab (Burns: *Halloween* 1785) a garter tied below the knee of a young man as a sign that he was about to make an offer of marriage

subarrhation (Swinburne: *Spousals* 1686) a betrothal accomplished by the man's showering presents on his incipient bride

acquaintance (Shropshire) a fiancé/e

maiden-rent (17C) a fee paid by every tenant in the Welsh manor of Builth at their marriage (given to the lord for his omitting the ancient custom of **marcheta**, whereby he spent the first night with his tenant's new wife)

gluepot (b.1811) a parson (from joining men and women together in matrimony)

IN THE PAPERS

In the UK, people of a certain class have traditionally advertised marriage, just as they do births and deaths, with an announcement in their newspaper of choice. This trio defining a person's life is colloquially known as **hatched, matched and dispatched** (with some believing that these really are the only times your name should appear in the papers). In Australia, similar announcements are known as **yells, bells and knells**. But though established through long custom, marriage has come in many varied and interesting forms ...

paranymph (1660) the best man or bridesmaid at a wedding
levirate (1725) the custom requiring a man to marry his brother's widow
punalua (1889) a group marriage in which wives' sisters and husbands' brothers were considered spouses
adelphogamy (1926) a form of marriage in which brothers share a wife or wives
jockum-gagger (1797) a man living on the prostitution of his wife
bitch's blind (US slang) a wife who acts as a cover for a homosexual male
opsigamy (1824) marrying late in life

VIRAGO

Maritality (1812) is a charming word, meaning 'the excessive affection a wife feels for her husband', while **levament** (1623) describes one of the best aspects of a good marriage, 'the comfort a man has from his wife'. But in general the words and phrases our language has thrown up speak of more demanding realities, with wives all too often in the frame:

loudspeaker (underworld slang 1933) a wife
alarm clock (US slang 1920s) a nagging woman
tenant at will (late 18C) one whose wife arrives at the alehouse to make him come home
ten commandments (mid 15C) the ten fingers and thumbs especially of a wife
curtain-lecture (b.1811) a reproof given by a wife to her husband in bed
cainsham smoke (1694) the tears of a man who is beaten by his wife (deriving from a lost story relating to Keynsham, near Bristol)

AFTERPLAY

Love and marriage, the song goes, go together 'like horse and carriage'. So why doesn't fidelity always fit so easily into the equation?

wittol (15C) a man who is aware of his wife's unfaithfulness but doesn't mind or acquiesces

court of assistants (late 18C) the young men with whom young wives, unhappy in their marriages to older men, are likely to seek solace

to pick a needle without an eye (West Indian) of a young woman, to give oneself in marriage to a man whom one knows will be of no use as a sexual partner

gandermooner (1617) a husband who strays each month, during the time of the month when his wife is 'unavailable'

stumble at the truckle-bed (mid 17C) to 'mistake' the maid's bed for one's wife's

UP THE DUFF

The desire to expand the family is all too natural; though the actual circumstances of conception may vary considerably:

beer babies (Sussex) babies sired when the man was drunk

Band-Aid baby (UK slang) a child conceived to strengthen a faltering relationship

basting (UK slang 2007) being with a gay male friend who offers to give the baby a woman longs for

sooterkin (1658) an imaginary kind of birth attributed to Dutch women from sitting over their stoves

THE STORK DESCENDS

In parts of America they say you have **swallowed a watermelon seed** when you become pregnant. In Britain, children were once told that the new baby boy in the family had been found **under the gooseberry bush**, while the girl was found **in the parsley bed**:

omphalomancy (1652) divination by counting the knots in the umbilical cord of her first born to predict the number of children a mother will have
nom de womb (US slang 2005) a name used by an expectant parent to refer to their unborn child
infanticipate (US 1934) to be expecting a child
quob (b.1828) to move as the embryo does in the womb; as the heart does when throbbing
pigeon pair (Wiltshire dialect) a boy and a girl (when a mother has only two children)

PRIVATE VIEWS

As soon as Baby appears, of course, there is much excitement. Relatives and friends crowd round to check out the new arrival, and any gossip about the timing of the pregnancy melts away:

barley-child (Shropshire) a child born in wedlock, but which makes its advent within six months of marriage (alluding to the time which elapses between barley sowing and barley harvest)
jonkin (Yorkshire) a tea-party given to celebrate a birth of a child
crying-cheese (Scotland) a ritual where cheese was given to neighbours and visitors when a child was born

FIRST STEPS

Then there is the long, slow process of bringing up the little darling; beset with many dangers, but not, fortunately, as many as in the past . . .

vagitus (Latin 17C) a new-born child's cry
marriage music (late 17C) the crying of children
blow-blow (Jamaican English 1955) babbling baby-talk
chrisom (*c.*1200) a child that dies within a month of its birth (so called from the chrisom-cloth, anointed with holy unguent, which the children wore until they were christened)
quiddle (Midlands) to suck a thumb
gangrel (1768) a child just beginning to walk
dade (Shropshire) to lead children when learning to walk

CHIPS OFF THE OLD BLOCK

It's an exhausting time, but hopefully rewarding, whatever the extra commitments:

antipelargy (1656) the love of children for their parents
philostorgy (1623) natural affection, such as that between parents and children
butter-print (Tudor–Stuart) a child bearing the stamp of its parents' likeness
stand pad (Cockney) to beg in crowded streets with a written statement round one's neck, such as 'wife and five kids to support'
sandwich generation (Canadian slang) those caring for young children and elderly parents at the same time (usually 'baby boomers' in their 40s or 50s)

POPPING OFF

Sadly, not all men seem able to stay the course:

zoo daddy (US slang) a divorced father who rarely sees his child or children (he takes his kids to the zoo when exercising his visiting rights)

baby fathers (Jamaican English 1932) males who abandon their partner and offspring

goose father (US slang 2005) a father who lives alone having sent his spouse and children to a foreign country to learn English or do some other form of advanced study

jacket (Jamaican English 2007) a man tested and proven not to be the father of the children said to be his

EARLY PROMISE

And what a course it can prove to be . . .

glaikut (Aberdeenshire) of a child too fond of its mother and refusing to be parted from her at any time

chippie-burdie (Scotland) a promise made to a child to pacify them

killcrop (1652) a child who is perpetually hungry

vuddle (Hampshire and Wiltshire) to spoil a child by injudicious petting

ankle-sucker (Worcestershire) a child or person dependent on others

COLTISH

Not necessarily made any easier as the offspring grow older . . .

dandiprat (1583) an urchin
daddle (Suffolk) to walk like a young child trying to copy its father
liggle (East Anglian) to carry something too heavy to be carried easily (e.g. of a child with a puppy)
airling (1611) a person who is both young and thoughtless

. . . though getting them outside in the fresh air is always a good plan . . .

grush (Hiberno-English) of children, to scramble for coins and other small gifts thrown at them
duck's dive (Newfoundland) a boy's pastime of throwing a stone into the water without making a splash
poppinoddles (Cumberland 1885) a boyish term for a somersault
triltigo (Derbyshire) a word used to start boys off in a race
treer (*c.*1850) a boy who avoids organized sports, but plays a private game with one or two friends (by the trees at the side of the ground)

ABC

School can take some of the heat off the parents . . .

abecedary (1440) a table or book containing the alphabet, a primer
minerval (1603) a gift given in gratitude by a pupil to a teacher
brosier (Eton College *c.*1830) a boy with no more pocket money
nix! (1860) a warning especially among schoolboys and workmen of somebody's approach

MANNERS MAKYTH MAN

At Winchester College, as elsewhere in times gone by, discipline was strictly maintained by corporal punishment. If it wasn't from the authorities, you could count on the bullies for trouble:

tin gloves (*c.*1840) a criss-cross of blisters methodically made by a bully on the back of a victim's hand

bibler (*c.*1830) six cuts on the back

tund (1831) to flog a boy across the shoulders with a ground-ash

rabbiter (1831) a blow on the back of their neck with the edge of the open palm

to sport eyesight (1920) to deliver all the blows on the same spot in beating

FIGHTING YOUR BATTELS

Similar slang was adopted at many universities. At Oxford, your **battels** (Tudor–Stuart) were (and still are) your college bills; if you didn't get to an exam you **ploughed** (1853) it; and **academic nudity** (b.1909) was appearing in public without a cap or gown. At Cambridge, in Victorian times, a **brute** (19C) was one who had not matriculated and a **sophister** (1574) was an undergraduate in his second or third year. In both places a **whiffler** (*c.*1785) was one who examined candidates for degrees, while at Dublin a **sizar** (1588) was one who got a college allowance. At Aberdeen, from the eighteenth century on, you were a **bajan** in your first year, a **semi** in your second, a **tertian** in your third, and a **magistrand** (1721) if staying for a fourth year to sit an MA.

JUST MISSED A GEOFF

Much more recently, a new slang has grown up to describe the various kinds of degrees that one may hope to get. The much-prized First has been known as a **Geoff** (Hurst), a **Damien** (Hirst) or a **Patty** (Hearst), a **raging** (thirst) or a **James** (the First). A 2:1 is known as an **Attila** (the Hun) or a **Made-In** (Taiwan). A 2:2 is known as a **Desmond** (Tutu) and a Third as a **Douglas** (Hurd), a **Thora** (Hird), or even a **Gentleman's Degree,** though who would admit to having one of those these days?

RETURN TO THE COOP

Education over, for more than a few the appeal of moving back home can be strong, especially in these days of high rents and generous parental expectations:

twixters (US slang) fully grown men and women who still live with their parents

ant hill family (UK slang) the trend whereby children move back in with their parents so that all can work together towards group financial goals

LIFE IS SHORT

Life races on, and all too soon comes that point when some feel the need to start lying about their age . . .

agerasia (1706) looking younger than one really is
paracme (1656) the point at which one's prime is past
menoporsche (UK slang) the phenomenon of middle-aged men attempting to recapture their lost youth by buying an expensive sports car

. . . a pointless activity, for your years will always catch up with you:

prosopagnosia (1950) an inability to recognize familiar faces
sew the button on (UK slang b.1898) to have to jot down at once what you wish to remember
astereognosis (1900) the loss of the ability to recognize the shapes and spatial relationships of objects

WORD JOURNEYS

debonair (13C from Old French: de bonne aire) of good disposition or family
puny (16C from Old French: puis né) born later, a junior; then inexperienced
husband (Old English) master of a house; then (13C) husbandman: tiller of the soil (an extension of his duties); then (15C) housekeeper or steward; then (16C) a man who managed affairs generally

OYSTER PARTS
Culture

Literature should be my staff
but not my crutch

(Scott: *Lockhart's Life* 1830)

There's little doubt that as a culture we have a passion for a good story well told:

anecdotard (1894) an old man given to telling stories
ackamarackus (US slang 1934) a specious, characteristically involved tale that seeks to convince by bluff
SHAZAM (1940) Solomon's wisdom, Hercules' strength, Atlas's stamina, Zeus's power, Achilles' courage and Mercury's speed (an acronymic magic word like 'abracadabra' used to introduce an extraordinary story)
shark-jump (US media jargon 1997) instances that signal the imminent decline of a TV series by introducing plot twists inconsistent with the previous plot
bridges, bridges! (*c.*1880) a cry to arrest a long-winded story

THE BEST WORDS IN THE BEST ORDER

Poetry too seems to be in the blood, and judging by the activity in pubs around the nation, in no danger of declining:

genethliacon (1589) a poem written for someone's birthday
amphigory (1809) a poem that seems profound but is nonsense
randle (b.1811) a set of nonsensical verses, repeated in Ireland by schoolboys and young people, who have been guilty of breaking wind backwards before their companions
rhapsodomancy (1727) fortunetelling by picking a passage of poetry at random
musophobist (Swinburne 1880) a person who regards poetry with suspicious dislike

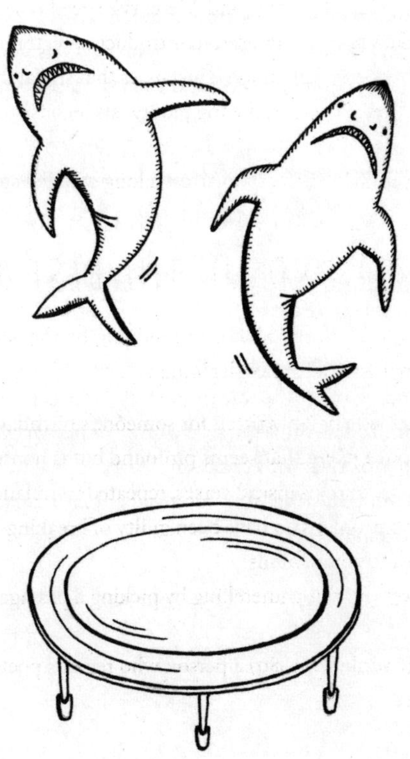

PENMEN

Scribblers still throng a land where people have long been under the illusion that there is something glamorous about the business of writing:

purlicue (1808) a dash or flourish at the end of a written word
wegotism (1797) the excessive use of 'we' in writing (particularly in newspaper editorials)
parisology (1846) the use of ambiguous language or evasive writing
macaronic (1638) mixing words from different languages
Patavinity (1607) the use of local slang or expressions when writing
cloak-father (*c.*1639) a pretended author whose name is put forth to conceal the real author

CRITICAL MASS

The best advice for authors is Somerset Maugham's: 'Don't read your reviews, dear boy. Measure them'...

Zoilist (1594) a critic, especially one who is unduly severe or who takes joy in faultfinding (after the fourth-century Greek critic)
histriomastix (Tudor–Stuart) a severe critic of playwrights
squabash (1818) to crush with criticism
praise sandwich (US slang Houston 1987) criticism prefaced by and followed by compliments

BOOKS DO FURNISH A ROOM

There remains one important group that no one in the business can afford to take for granted – the dear old readers:

enchiridion (Late Latin 1541) a book carried in the hand for reference
thumbscall (Shropshire) a piece of paper or card inserted in a book to mark a page
bibliotaph (1824) a person keeping his or her books secret or locked up
grille-peerer (1940s) one of a group of clergymen who used to haunt the stacks of the London Library to look up the skirts of women browsing above
to have a face-ticket (British Museum Reading Room 1909) to be so well known to the janitors that one is not asked to present one's ticket

ARE YOU WORKING?

Sitting in a corner with a mere book has never been enough for another creative group who flourish in our supposedly inhibited culture:

oyster part an actor who appears and speaks or acts only once (like an oyster he opens but once)
nap-nix (*c.*1860) an amateur playing minor parts for experience
crawk (1930s) a performer acting as an animal imitator
cabotinage (1894) behaviour typical of a second-rate actor or strolling player, implying a tendency to play to the gallery or overact
come back Tuesday pseudo-friendly advice from theatrical directors and management to hopefuls really meaning 'go away!'
flag-fallen (16C) unemployed (used first of actors: the playhouse flag was lowered where there was no performance)

AGAIN FROM THE TOP

Many are the tricks of the trade to be learnt in this most demanding of callings; and theatre has developed a fine jargon to describe it:

swallow the cackle to learn a part
ping to speak one's lines softly, with no special emphasis
pong to speak in blank verse after forgetting one's lines
stagger the first rehearsal without a script in one's hands
wing to fasten one's script to one of the wing flats or some part of the scenery when one has failed to learn it properly and thus needs an occasional reference during the performance
Mummerset (J. B. Priestley: *Festival at Farbridge* 1951) fake peasant accents adopted by actors to denote a supposed rural origin (from a mix of Somerset and mummer)

SMOKE AND MIRRORS

Normal costume apart, a range of cunning accessories assist the thespian's art:

heart the padding out of their tights by acrobats, actors etc. to prevent an otherwise painful fall
wafters (Geordie) swords made with blunt edges for performers
bronteon (Ancient Greek 1849) a device used in theatre or movies to create thunder
scruto (1853) a spring trap-door, flush with the floor of a stage, for a ghost to rise through, for sudden falls and other effects
pepper's ghost a trick used to create a 'ghost' on stage by using an inclined sheet of plate glass onto which an actor can be projected as if 'walking through air'
bird's nest crepe wool used to construct false beards

LIGHTS UP

But once you're out there, darling, all you can do is stick to the script and hope for the best:

ventilator a play so appallingly bad that the audience leaves well before the final curtain, and their seats are filled only with fresh air
exsibilation (1640) the collective hisses of a disapproving audience
handcuffed an actor's description of an audience who will not applaud
stiff (1930s) a terrible joke, rewarded only by silence
soso (1930s) a joke rewarded by a smile, but not a laugh
gravy easy laughs from a friendly audience
crack the monica (music hall jargon *c.*1860) to ring the bell to summon a performer to reappear

BUMS ON SEATS

Though you may be deep into your role, you'll still have one eye on the view beyond the footlights:

plush family empty seats in the auditorium (i.e. the plush-covered seats that can be seen from the stage)
paper the house to give away free theatre tickets in order to fill up an undersubscribed performance
whiskey seats seats on the aisle (popular both with critics, who need to get out before the rush and phone in their reviews, and those who like to escape to the bar when the action palls)
baskets are in a full house (from the one-time practice of leaving the prop baskets as security against the income of a touring company: if the house didn't guarantee the payment of the theatre's rent, the props were theoretically forfeit)

MAGIC CIRCLE

But let's please never forget that the stage is not simply a venue for actors. Other fine artists offer equally enjoyable entertainment:

burn (conjuring jargon) staring at the magician's hands without averting your gaze, no matter what misdirection is thrown
riffle (conjuring jargon) to let cards come out of the hand, creating a noise
grimoire (French 1849) a magician's manual of black magic for invoking demons
cultrivorous (1846) actual or illusory knife-swallowing
drollic (1743) pertaining to a puppet show
swazzle (1942) a mouthpiece used by a puppeteer to make the squeaking voice of Mr Punch

MORE WHIFFLE

Other performers don't even need a stage. From break to Morris dance, a pavement or floor is more than enough:

gaff a dancer's belt, the protection under his tights for his genitals
garlic (17C) a lively jig
applejack (1980s) a basic move to challenge another breakdancer to a competition, squatting down, falling back onto your hands, and kicking one leg high in the air, then springing back onto both legs
whiffler the man with the whip in Morris dancing

CROONERS

Singers, too, can operate anywhere:

griddle (b.1851) to sing in the streets
woodshedding (1976) spontaneous barbershop singing (originally meaning a place to rehearse music privately)
barcarole (French 1779) a gondolier's song
rumbelow (1315) a meaningless song or refrain sung by sailors while rowing a boat (e.g. Heave Ho or Hey-Ho)
aubade (Franco-Provençal 1678) a song at sunrise
scolion (Ancient Greek 1603) a song sung in turn by the guests at a banquet

ROCK FOLLIES

Though why be a busker when you could be a star? Or at least get as near to one as possible . . .

guerrilla gig a performance by a band in an unlikely venue, where they play until they are evicted
mosh to engage in uninhibited, frenzied activities with others near the stage at a rock concert (**mosh pit** the place near the stage at a rock concert where moshing occurs)
wollyhumper a bouncer employed by a rock band to make sure no fans manage to climb on stage while they play or, if they have climbed up, to throw them down again
résumé on a rope a backstage pass
woodpecker people who nod their heads to the music being played while paying no attention

GOGGLE BOX

There is one contemporary venue where almost all performers are happy to be seen; and behind the scenes in TV land, too, a whole rich lingo has grown up:

toss in television news, an onscreen handover from one host to another
golden rolodex the small handful of experts who are always quoted in news stories and asked to be guests on discussion shows
bambi someone who freezes in front of the camera (like a deer caught in headlights)
clambake the possibility of two or three commentators all talking over each other and thus confusing listeners
goldfishing one politician talking inaudibly in an interview (you can see his lips move but only hear the reporter's words)

WORD JOURNEYS

explode (16C from Latin) to reject; then (17C) to drive out by clapping, to hiss off the stage
tragedy (16C from Ancient Greek) a goat song
anecdote (from Ancient Greek) unpublished things; then (17C) secret history
charm (from Latin carmen) a song; then (13C) an incantation, the singing or reciting of a verse that was held to have magic power
enthusiasm (from Ancient Greek) divinely inspired; then (17C) possession by a god, poetic frenzy; misguided religious emotion

DIMBOX AND QUOCKERWODGER

Military and political concerns

Soldiers in peace are like
chimneys in summer

(1598)

We all claim to love a peaceful time, but somehow squabbles keep breaking out:

breed-bate (1593) someone looking for an argument
conspue (1890) to spit on someone or something with contempt
cobble-nobble (Shropshire) to rap on the head with the knuckles
donnybrook (1852) a street brawl (named after the famously violent annual Fair in Dublin)
recumbentibus (b.1546) a knock-down blow either verbal or physical
sockdolager (1830) a decisive blow or answer that settles a dispute

SHADOW DANCING

Fights come in all shapes and sizes:

batrachomyomachy (b.1828) a silly and trifling altercation (literally, a battle between frogs and mice)
sciamachy (1623) fighting with a shadow or with an imaginary enemy
holmgang (1847) a duel to the death fought on an island
ro-sham-bo (US slang 1998) a competition employed to determine the ownership of an object when in dispute (the two parties kick each other in the groin until one falls to the ground: the person left standing wins)
hieromachy (1574) a conflict of ecclesiastics, a fight between persons of the cloth

... and brave the person who tries to come between the opposing parties:

dimbox (Scotland) the 'smoother-over' of disputes, an expert at getting others to make up
redder's lick (Scott: *The Abbot* 1820) the blow one receives in trying to part combatants
autoclaps (Jamaican English 1970s) trouble that leads to more trouble

GOING REGIMENTAL

When it comes to the bigger disagreements between nations, we still, it seems, need armies to protect us – the perfect breeding ground for specialized lingo and tradition:

boots (b.1811) the youngest officer in a regimental mess, whose duty it is to **skink** (b.1811) to stir the fire, snuff any candles and ring the bell
militaster (1640) a soldier without military skill or knowledge
egg (early 20C) an inexperienced airman, not yet 'hatched'
knapsack descent (late 19C) a soldier or soldiers in every generation of a family
alvarado (Tudor–Stuart) the rousing of soldiers at dawn by beating the drum or the firing of a gun
yomp (1982) to march with heavy equipment over difficult terrain; a forced military march in full kit

YELLOW-BELLY

Not that everyone is equally eager to join the battle:

murcous (1684) of one who cuts off his thumb to escape military service
troppo (Australian slang) nervously affected by the privations of war service in the Tropics
ear-flip (Service slang) a very cursory salute
chamade (French 1684) the drum beat or trumpet blast which announces a surrender
poodle-faker (Service slang 1902) an officer always ready to take part in the social side of military life

WEIGHING ANCHOR

The navy, too, has developed some colourful jargon over the years:

anchor-faced someone, usually an officer, who lives and breathes the Royal Navy even when retired

mushroom troop a complaining description used by those who feel that they are not being told enough about what is happening (i.e. fed on dirt and kept in the dark)

Dockyard Olympics the old process of refitting a warship whereby all the tradesmen lined up at the start of the day and then raced off to various places within the ship

upstairs (submariner's jargon) the surface of the sea

swallow the anchor to leave the navy

MAGNIFICENT MEN

Our newest military service was at first rather looked down on by the other two. But it didn't take long to prove its usefulness:

spike-bozzle (1915) to destroy (an enemy plane)
bombflet (New Zealand 1940) a propaganda leaflet dropped from an aeroplane
brolly-hop (b.1932) a parachute jump
vrille (French 1918) an aerobatic spinning manoeuvre (twisting, like the tendril of a vine)

Whatever the difficulties...

socked in (aerospace jargon) an airfield shut for flying because of poor visibility
penguin (Air Force jargon 1915) an aeroplane unable to leave the ground
dangle the Dunlops (Royal Navy jargon) to lower an aircraft's undercarriage prior to landing

or the dangers...

cigarette roll (US slang 1962) a parachute jump in which the parachute fails to open
angry palm tree (Royal Navy jargon) a burning and turning helicopter
buy the farm (US Service slang 1955) to crash an aircraft, usually fatally (referring to government compensation paid to a farmer when an aircraft crashes on his farm)

at least it had its compensations:

modoc(k) (US slang 1936) a man who becomes a pilot for the sake of the glamorous image it conveys

SHOCK AND AWE

As the airforce role becomes ever more important, and the machines more powerful and hi-tech, the lingo just keeps on coming:

green air (US slang) flying with night-vision goggles

play pussy (RAF jargon) to fly into cloud cover in order to avoid being discovered by hostile aircraft

glass ball environment (US intelligence jargon 2004) of the weather in Iraq being often conducive to collecting images from above

PANCAKE! – SERVICES' WATCHWORDS

popeye! (air intercept code) I am in cloud; I have reduced visibility

state tiger! (air intercept code) 'I have sufficient fuel to complete my mission as assigned'

Geronimo! (1940s) the favoured shout of paratroopers as they leapt from airplanes

Pancake! (Service slang) the order given in the air to land

lumpy chicken! (US military use) loud and clear

SPOOKS

Our fourth service lurks in the shadows, complete with its own covert terms of communication:

cut-out someone acting as a middle-man in espionage

starburst losing a tail by having several similar cars suddenly drive off in different directions, making it hard to know which to follow

swallow a woman employed by the Soviet intelligence service to seduce men for the purposes of espionage

lion tamer in a blackmail operation, a strong-arm man who makes sure that the target, once told that he is being blackmailed, does not make an embarrassing and potentially destructive fuss which could thus ruin the operation

ill arrested on suspicion for questioning

demote maximally to kill one of your associates (the victim's career as a spy certainly can fall no lower)

POLITICOS

We can only hope that all these fine operatives are given wise and honourable direction by that class of men and women we choose to run things for us:

tyrekicker (New Zealand 1986) a politician who discusses and debates but takes no action (from car sales where a person examines a car at length but does not buy it)

snollygoster (1846) a burgeoning politician (especially a shrewd or calculating one) with no platform, principles or party preference

dog-whistle politics (Australian slang 2005) to present your message so that only your supporters hear it properly

quockerwodger (mid 19C) a pseudo-politician; a politician acting in accordance with the instructions of an influential third party, rather than properly representing their constituents (a quockerwodger was a wooden toy figure which, when pulled by a string, jerked its limbs about)

moss-back (late 19C) a right-winger (as they move so slowly that moss could grow on their back)

doughnutting (UK slang 2005) a carefully created seating plan which places an ideal group of members of Parliament (women, photogenic, ethnic minority etc.) around a leader for the ideal television shot

mugwump (New York 1884) one who holds more or less aloof from party politics, professing disinterested and superior views

girouettism (1825) frequently altering one's opinions or principles to follow trends

TWO CHEERS FOR DEMOCRACY

We live, after all, in the finest political system yet devised by man:

pot-waller (Somerset) one whose right to vote for a member of Parliament is based on his having a fireplace on which to boil his own pot

flusher (US slang 2008) a volunteer who rounds up non-voters on Election Day

astroturfing (US slang) a PR tactic in which hired acolytes are used to offer ostensibly enthusiastic and spontaneous grassroots support for a politician or business

barbecue stopper (Australian slang 2002) an issue of major public importance, which will excite the interest of voters

WORD JOURNEYS

opportune (15C from Latin via Old French) (of wind) driving towards the harbour; seasonable

bounce (13C) to beat, thump; then (16C) a loud, exploding noise

borough (Old English) a fortress

the devil to pay (1783) from the time of old sailing ships when the devil was a long seam beside the keel of a ship which was sealed with tar (if there was no hot pitch ready the tide would turn before the work could be done and the ship would be out of commission longer)

SCURRYFUNGE

Domestic life

A lyttle house well fylled,
a lytle ground well tylled and
a little wife well wylled
is best

(1545)

Pundits talk of the global village, but the world is still a huge and deeply varied place, offering any number of environments for people to settle in:

Periscii (1625) the inhabitants of the polar circles, so called because in summer their shadows form an oval

Ascians (1635) inhabitants of the Tropics, who twice a year have the sun directly overhead at noon (hence 'without shadows')

antiscian (1842) a person who lives on the opposite side of the Equator

epirot (1660) a person who lives inland

paralian (1664) a person who lives near the sea

owd standards (Lincolnshire) old folk who have lived in a village all their lives

carrot cruncher (UK slang) a person from the country, a rural dweller

BRIGHT LIGHTS

Countryside, town or something in between, take your pick:

agroville (1960) a community, a village stronghold (relating to South Vietnam)
tenderloin district (1887) the area of a city devoted to pleasure and entertainment, typically containing restaurants, theatres, gambling houses and brothels
huburb (US slang) its own little city within another city

HIGHLY SOUGHT AFTER

Local features may add to or subtract from the desirability of one's residence:

hippo's tooth (US slang) a cement bollard
witches' knickers (Irish slang) shopping bags caught in trees, flapping in the wind
urbeach (US slang) an urban beach generally built along a riverbank
generica (US slang) features of the American landscape (strip malls, motel chains, prefab housing) that are exactly the same no matter where one is
packman's puzzle (Wales) a street or housing estate where the house numbers are allocated in a complicated fashion which causes problems to visitors, tradesmen etc.

SOILED BY ASSOCIATION

If you stay too long in one place you might saddle your children with a nickname they never asked for:

beanbelly (17C) a native of Leicestershire (a major producer of beans)
malt-horse (17C) a native of Bedford (from the high-quality malt extracted from Bedfordshire barley)
yellow belly (18C) a native of Lincolnshire (especially of the southern or fenland part where the yellow-stomached frog abounds)

LOVE THY NEIGHBOUR

It's generally wisest to try and meet the neighbours before you actually move in; though the horrid truth is that the people next door can change at any time:

baching (New Zealand 1936) living usually apart from a family and without domestic help, 'doing for oneself' (especially of a male)
scurryfunge (coastal American 1975) a hasty tidying of the house between the time you see a neighbour and the time she knocks on the door
exhibition meal (Hobo slang) a handout eaten on the doorstep: the madam wants the neighbours to witness her generosity
flying pasty (*c.*1790) excrement wrapped in paper that is thrown over a neighbour's wall
to have the key of the street (b.1881) of a person who has no house to go to at night, or is shut out from his own

HOUSEPROUD

Once you've settled in, though, you're free to make what you like of the rooms . . .

piggery (UK college slang early 20C) a room in which one does just as one wishes and which is rarely cleaned
chambradeese (Scotland) the best bedroom
ruelle (Tudor–Stuart) the space in a bedroom between the bed and the wall
but and ben (Geordie) outside and inside (refers to a two-roomed house with an outer and inner room)

though you're all too likely to become swamped in the details of domesticity:

flisk (Gloucestershire) a brush to remove cobwebs
izels (Lincolnshire) particles of soot floating about in a room, indicating that the chimney needs to be swept
beggar's velvet (1847) downy particles which accumulate under furniture from the negligence of housemaids
winter-hedge (Yorkshire 18C) a clothes-horse (from the way a full clothes-horse 'hedged off' a portion of a room: summer washing was dried out of doors)
wemble (Lincolnshire) to invert a basin or saucepan on a shelf so that dust does not settle on the inside
poss (Shropshire) to splash up and down in the water, as washerwomen do when rinsing their clothes

ust make sure you don't take it so far that that you upset your cohabitants . . .

spannel (Sussex) to make dirty foot marks on a clean floor
heel (Gloucestershire) to upset a bucket
spang (Lincolnshire) to shut a door by flicking the handle sharply so that it slams without being held

HOUSEWARMING

With the place spick and span, perhaps it's time to throw that party:

tin-kettling (New Zealand 1874) a house-warming custom whereby a newly wed couple were welcomed by friends and neighbours circling the marriage home banging on kerosene tins until provided with refreshments

cuddle puddle (New York slang 2002) a heap of exhausted ravers

buff-ball (1880) a party where everyone dances naked

THE THREE NIGHT RULE

A well-known proverb says that fish and guests go off after three nights, so if you ask people to stay for longer, make sure you have some way of getting rid of them if need be:

thwertnick (Old English law) entertaining a sheriff for three nights
agenhina (Saxon law) a guest at an inn who, after having stayed for three nights, was considered one of the family
sit eggs (US black slang 1970s) to overstay one's welcome (from the image of a hen awaiting her chicks)

BATHTIME

Because, in the end, what could be nicer than closing the front door to all outsiders and taking the relaxing ablution of your choice:

offald (Yorkshire) tired and dirty, in need of a bath
muck-rawk (Yorkshire) a dirty line (e.g. on neck) showing the limit of where it has been washed
cowboy (US slang) a quick bath using little water (since cowboys bathed sparingly)
psychrolutist (1872) one who bathes in the open air daily throughout the winter

BEDDY-BYES

Before sinking into a well-deserved rest, wherever in the house the fancy takes you:

nid-nod (1787) to nod off
counting rivets (Royal Navy jargon) going to sleep: it refers to lying down and looking at the rivets above the bunk
hypnopompic (1901) the fuzzy state between being awake and asleep
to sleep in puppy's parlour (Newfoundland 1771) to sleep on the floor in one's clothes
bodkin (1638) a person wedged in between two others when there is proper room for two only (a bodkin was a small sharp dagger)
admiral's watch (underworld slang 1905) a good night's sleep, especially at night
to drive one's pigs to market (US 19C) to snore

WORD JOURNEYS

detect (15C from Latin) to unroof
climax (from Ancient Greek) a ladder; then (16C) in rhetoric, an ascending series of expressions
curfew (13C from Old French: couvre feu) to cover the fire

AW WHOOP

Animals

You may beat a horse till he be sad,
and a cow till she be mad

(1678)

In a world where dogs are unclean in some cultures and on the menu in others, the British Isles is one place where the life of the average mutt might not be so bad:

snuzzle (1861) to poke around with one's nose, as dogs do
flew (1575) the pendulous corner of the upper lip of certain dogs, such as the bloodhound
lill (Gloucestershire) used of the tongue of a dog dropping his saliva
slink (Shropshire) to draw back, as a dog does when about to bite
pudding (underworld slang 1877) liver drugged for the silencing of house-dogs
ar dawg's a sooner (Ulster) my dog prefers to pee on the carpet rather than go outside

GRIMALKIN

Our other favourite domestic animal is supposed to have nine lives and knows how to enjoy all of them:

ess-rook (Shropshire) a cat that likes to lie in the ashes on the hearth
tawl-down (Somerset) to smooth down a cat's back
brebit (Shropshire) a cat that continually hunts for food
furs bush (Sussex) the cat's tune when purring

PRANCERS AND DOBBINS

The Queen is said to prefer horses to people, and there's little doubt they get to mix in the best company:

fossple (Cumberland 1783) the impression of a horse's hoof upon soft ground
trizzling (Devon) the slow, lazy trot of horses
brills (1688) a horse's eyelashes
skewboglish (Lincolnshire) a horse that is apt to shy
reeaster (Yorkshire) a horse making less effort than the others in a team
feague (UK slang b.1811) to put ginger or a live eel into a horse's anus to make him lively and carry his tail well
jipping (horsetraders' slang mid 19C) staining part of a horse with Indian ink to conceal a blemish

LIVESTOCK

It's all very well going to the races, but where would we be without the milk and cheese from our herds of Jerseys and Guernseys (to say nothing of the beef from Herefords, Galloways and Lincolns)?

ganners (Shetland Isles) the inside of a cow's lips
noit (Yorkshire) the period during which a cow gives milk
tulchan (1789) calf's skin set beside a cow to make her give milk freely
shick (Caithness) to set the head as a bull does when intending to toss
giddhom (Ireland) the frantic galloping of cows plagued with flies

LAND OF THE LONG WHITE FLEECE

Sheep are the animal most mentioned in the bible (lions and lambs came in second and third). In New Zealand, where there have long been more sheep than people, a whole separate language grew up for talking about them:

break back (1864) to run or dash in the reverse direction to the drive
pink (1897) to shear a sheep carefully and so closely that the skin shows
raddle (1910) to mark an unsatisfactorily shorn sheep
huntaway (1912) a noisy sheepdog trained to bark on command and drive sheep forward from behind
drummer (1897) the worst or slowest sheep-shearer in a team
cobbler (late 19C) the last and least willing sheep to be sheared

PORKER

In strong competition with the Danes, our hogs and sows do their level best to bring home the bacon:

hodge (Shropshire) the large paunch in a pig
wurtle (Cumberland) to work underneath or in the ground like a pig
treseltrype (Somerset 1883) the youngest in a litter of pigs

FOWL PLAY

Some birds we keep as hunters or pets, some we breed to mow down with guns, a few we eat . . .

turdoid (1823) akin to a thrush
ostreger (1400) a keeper of goshawks
hack (1575) eagles before they become acclimatized and can hunt on their own
ossiger (Orkney Isles) the condition of a fowl when moulting
jollop (1688) to gobble like a turkey
zoo-zoo (Gloucestershire) a wood pigeon (from the sound it makes)

. . . but they're always worth listening to:

quit-quit (Wiltshire 1900) the note of the swallow
quee-beck (Scotland 1901) the cry of grouse when startled
hoolie-gool-oo-oo (Banffshire 1876) the cry, hooting of an owl
valentine (1851) to greet with song at mating-time (said of birds)
chavish (1674) the sound of many birds chirping together, or many people chatting at once

QUEENS AND WORKERS

In other parts of the world they eat fried grasshopper and chocolate-coated ants; but with one glorious exception, insects are not much help in our national diet:

warp (Tudor–Stuart) bees in flight working themselves forward
cut (Gloucestershire) the second swarm of bees in the same season (**hob** or **kive**: the third swarm of bees)
spear (Sussex) the sting of a bee
narrow-wriggle (East Anglian) an earwig (the Yorkshire version is **forkin robins)**
dulosis (Modern Latin 1904) the enslavement of ants by ants

GREAT AND SMALL

The ordinary garden mole was known in Middle English (1100–1500) as a **mowdiwarp.** Later he became known as the **little gentleman in black velvet** (early 18C), the subject of a famous Jacobite toast to the mole that raised the hill that caused their oppressor King William to fall from his horse and die. Other animals have avoided such glorification . . .

fuz-pig (Somerset) a hedgehog
bubbly jock (Scottish) a turkey
pilser (b.1828) the moth or fly that runs into a candle flame

. . . but nonetheless their most obscure parts have been carefully noted . . .

junk (New Zealand 1837) the soft part of a sperm-whale's head
dewlap (1398) the pendulous skin under the throat of cattle, dogs etc.
cnidocil (1884) a stinging bristle of the tentacle of a jellyfish
katmoget (Shetland Isles 1897) having the colour of its belly different from the rest of the body

acnestis (1807) that part of an animal (between its shoulders and lower back) that it cannot reach to scratch
fleck (Essex) the soft hair of a rabbit

... not to mention their intriguing behaviours ...

mather (Gloucestershire) to turn round before lying down, as an animal often does
squeem (Ayrshire) the motion of a fish as observed by its effect on the surface of the water
pronk (1896) to leap through the air, as an antelope does
traffic (Gloucestershire) the tracks worn by rabbits or rats near their holes

... to say nothing of their mating habits ...

epigamic (1890) attracting the opposite sex at breeding time
clicket (b.1811) the copulation of foxes
amplexus (1930s) the mating embrace of a frog and a toad
caterwaul (Middle English) the cry of cats at mating time

YELLS BELLS

At rutting time a badger **shrieks** or **yells**; a boar **freams**; a buck **groans** or **troats**; a feret or stoat **chatters**; a fox **barks**; a goat **rattles**; a hare or rabbit **beats** or **taps**; a hart **bells**; an otter **whiles**; a roe **bellows** and a wold **howls**.

SAFETY IN NUMBERS

Most of us know that geese on the ground come in **gaggles.** But were you aware that when they take to the air they become a **skein**? The collective nouns for other animals are often bizarre in the extreme:

a **murder** of crows
a **watch** of nightingales
an **unkindness** of ravens
a **crash** of rhinoceroses
a **deceit** of lapwings
a **convocation** of eagles
a **business** of ferrets
a **wedge** of swans

JUG JUG IN BERKELEY SQUARE

When it comes to the sounds of animals, some of our attempts at mimicry may leave something to be desired:

curkle (1693) to cry as a quail
winx (15C) to bray like a donkey
desticate (1623) to squeak like a rat
chirr (1639) to make a trilling sound like a grasshopper
cigling (1693) chirping like the cicada
jug (1523) the sound of the nightingale
skirr (1870) a whirring or grating sound, as of the wings of birds in flight
gi'-me-trousers (Jamaican English 1958) the sound a cock makes when it crows

PEN AND INK

In Lincolnshire, the sounds of horses' hoofs were onomatopoeically described as **butter and eggs, butter and eggs** for a horse at a canter. If the animal happened to be a **clicker**, that is, it caught its front hoofs on its rear ones when it was running, there were extra beats in the rhythm and it went **hammer and pinchers, hammer and pinchers**. A horse at a gallop went **pen and ink, pen and ink**.

RUTH RUTH

And who knows how this strange variety of human calls to animals developed over the years?

muther-wut (Sussex) a carter's command to a horse to turn right
woor-ree (East Anglian 1893) a waggoner or ploughman's call to his horse to come to the right
harley-harther (Norfolk 1879) a call to horses to go to the left
aw whoop (Gloucestershire) an order for a horse to go on
fwyee (Northern) a peculiar noise made in speaking to a horse
rynt ye (Cheshire) what milkmaids say to their cows when they have milked them (similar to **aroint thee** – get ye gone)
ruth ruth (Ireland) an encouragement to a bull to service a cow
habbocraws (Scotland 1824) a shout used to frighten the crows from the cornfields
way leggo (New Zealand 1945) a musterer's cry to recall a dog
midda-whoy (Lincolnshire) an instruction to a horse to turn left

bumbeleery-bizz (Lanarkshire) a cry used by children when they see cows startling, in order to excite them to run about with greater violence

soho (1307) a call used by huntsmen to direct the attentions of a dog to a hare which has been discovered

whoo-up (Lancashire and Yorkshire 1806) a shout of huntsmen at the death of the quarry

poot, poot, poot (Orkney Isles) a call to young pigs at feeding time

cheddy-yow (Yorkshire) a call to sheep being brought down from the fell, to come closer

poa poa (Northamptonshire) a call to turkeys

tubby (Cornwall) a call used to pigeons

pleck-pleck (Scotland 1876) the cry of the oyster catcher

RSPCA

However good we are as a nation to our furry and feathered friends, there's certainly no room for complacency:

shangle (Cumbria) to fasten a tin or kettle to a dog's tail

hamble (1050) to make a dog useless for hunting by cutting the balls of its feet

brail (1828) the leather strap to bind a hawk's wing

gablock (1688) a spur attached to the heel of a fighting cock

bdellatomy (1868) the act of cutting a sucking leech to increase its suction

spanghew (1781) blowing up a frog through a straw inserted into its anus; the inflated frog was then jerked into the middle of the pond by being put on a cross stick, the other end being struck, so that it jumped high into the air

EXCREMENTAL

American slang has the phrase **alley** or **road apple** for a lump of horse manure. Back home in the Middle Ages the language of hunting meant that you didn't need slang to describe the specific faeces of an animal: there were the **crotels** of a hare, the **friants** of a boar, the **spraints** of an otter, the **werderobe** of a badger, the **waggying** of a fox and the **fumets** of a deer.

WORD JOURNEYS

mawkish (17C) from a maggot; nauseated

tabby (1630s) from Attabiyah, a quarter of Baghdad, renowned for its production of striped cloth

rostrum (16C from Latin) a bird's beak; then from the orator's platform in the Roman forum which was adorned with the prows of captured ships

white elephant (1851) from successive kings of Thailand who gave a white elephant to any courtier who irritated them; although the animals were considered sacred, their maintenance was so expensive that anyone who was given one was inevitably ruined

SWALLOCKY

Rural life and weather

Spring is here when you can
tread on nine daisies at once
on the village green

(1910)

Out in the sticks are things not dreamt of by those who remain in town:

goodman's croft (Scotland 19C) a corner of a field left untilled, in the belief that unless some such place were left, evil would befall the crop
loggers (Wiltshire) lumps of dirt on a ploughboy's feet
dudman (1674) a scarecrow made of old garments
icker (1513) a single ear of corn
squeaker (Newfoundland 1878) a blade of grass held upright between the thumbs and producing a shrill vibration when blown upon
cowpat roulette (Somerset 2004) a game in which villagers bet on which plot of land will be the first to receive a cow's calling card

FIGHTING FOR THE CLAICK

Dialects and local language identify particular aspects important to rural folk . . .

plud (Somerset) the swampy surface of a wet ploughed field
fleet (Somerset) the windward side of a hedge
wamflet (Aberdeenshire) the water of a mill stream, after passing the mill
chimp (Wiltshire) the grown-out shoot of a stored potato
griggles (Wiltshire) small worthless apples remaining on the tree after the crop has been gathered in

. . . as well as gadgets and techniques that have been developed over long years of experiment:

atchett (Devon and Cornwall) a pole slung across a stream to stop cattle passing
averruncator (1842) a long stick with shears for cutting high branches
stercoration (1605) the process of spreading manure
baggin-bill (Shropshire) an implement for reaping peas
reesome (Lincolnshire) to place peas in small heaps
claick (Scotland) the last armful of grain cut at harvest (also called the **kirn-cut, mulden**, or **kirn-baby**: it was often kept and hung by a ribbon above the fireplace; in Suffolk harvesters threw their sickles to compete to reap it)

GREEN FINGERS

On a smaller scale, gardeners always have plenty to talk about . . .

platiecrub (Shetland Isles) a patch of enclosed ground for growing cabbages
olitory (1658) belonging to the kitchen garden
chessom (1626) of soil; without stones or grit
pissabed (Jamaican English 1801) a dandelion (as it is a diuretic)

. . . and things can get pretty technical on occasion:

suckshin (Yorkshire) liquid manure
sarcle (1543) to dig up weeds with a hoe
graff (Shropshire) a spade's depth in digging (**delve** is two spades' depth)
cochel (Sussex) too much for a wheelbarrow but not enough for a cart

BOSKY

Out on the slopes beyond the hedge the trees too need careful categorizing:

maerapeldre (Anglo-Saxon) an apple-tree on a boundary
pollard (Newfoundland *c.*1900) a dead tree still standing
rampick (1593) a tree bare of leaves or twigs
stub-shot (Somerset) the portion of the trunk of a tree which remains when the tree is not sawn through

... and beyond that, Nature may be wilder and more magnificent still:

borstal (South English 1790) a pathway up to a steep hill
brucktummuck (Jamaican English 1943) a hill so steep that it seems to break the stomach of one who tries to climb it

UP ON THE DOWNS

Critics from abroad often claim that English weather is dreadful. But this is only one point of view; for others relish the huge variety of effects to be found in such a changeable climate. These are just those found in Sussex:

port-boys small low clouds in a clear sky
windogs white clouds blown by the wind
eddenbite a mass of cloud in the form of a loop
slatch a brief respite or interval in the weather
swallocky sultry weather
shucky unsettled weather
truggy dirty weather
egger-nogger sleet
smither diddles bright spots on either side of the sun

THE RAIN IT RAINETH EVERYDAY . . .

It may rain often but that's not to say that there aren't some happy aspects to the experience:

petrichor (1964) the pleasant smell that accompanies the first rain after a dry spell

eske (Orkney Isles) small spots of rain that precede a heavy storm

fog dog (mid 19C) the lower part of a rainbow

water-gall (Tudor–Stuart) a second rainbow seen above the first

monkey's wedding (South African 1968) simultaneous rain and sunshine

although its less enjoyable side is also well documented . . .

trashlifter (Californian slang) a heavy rain (**loglifter**: a really heavy rain)
duck's frost (Sussex dialect) cold rain rather than freezing
New York rain (Hong Kong slang) the local term for water that drips annoyingly from air-conditioners onto passers-by

BLOWN AWAY

For those who live on coasts and hills, the wind has always been a constant presence:

pipple (Tudor–Stuart) to blow with a gentle sound (of the wind)
wyvel (Wiltshire) to blow as wind does round a corner or through a hole
whiffle (1662) to blow, displace or scatter with gusts of air; to flicker or flutter as if blown by the wind

not to be trifled with if you're out on the water . . .

williwaw (1842) a sudden and powerful downdraught of wind (originally in the Straits of Magellan)
the dog before its master (nautical late 19C) a heavy swell preceding a gale

or a storm is imminent . . .

brattle (Newcastle 1815) the noise of a thunderclap
rounce robble hobble (b.1582) a representation of the tumult of thunder
heofonwoma (Anglo-Saxon) thunder and lightning, literally a terrible noise from heaven
levin (13C) a bolt of lightning

THE LIVING IS EASY

Every now and then the sun appears, and everyone goes crazy with delight:

apricate (1691) to bask in the sun
crizzles (1876) rough, sunburnt places on the face and hands in scorching weather
jack-a-dandy (Shropshire) the dancing light sometimes seen on a wall or ceiling, reflected from the sunshine on water, glass or other bright surface
king's-weather (Scotland 19C) the exhalations seen rising from the earth during a warm day (while **queen's weather** (18C) is a fine day for a fête as Queen Victoria was famous for having fine weather when she appeared in public)

SNOW ON THE LINE

While at the other end of the year the country grinds to a halt for another reason:

devil's blanket (Newfoundland) a snowfall which hinders work or going to school
pitchen (Bristol) snow that is settling
cloggins (Cumberland) balls of snow on the feet
tewtle (Yorkshire) to snow just a few flakes
sluppra (Shetland Isles) half-melted snow

although the novelty does often rather pass after the building of the second snowman:

two thieves beating a rogue (b.1811) a man beating his hands against his sides to warm himself in cold weather (also known as **beating the booby** and **cuffing Jonas**)
to beat the goose (*c*.1880) to strike the hands across the chest and under the armpits to warm one's chilled fingers (the movement supposedly resembles a goose in flight)
shrammed (Bristol) feeling really cold

WORD JOURNEYS

aftermath (16C) after mowing (i.e. the second crop of grass in autumn)

derive (14C from Latin via Old French) to draw away from the river bank

damp (14C) noxious vapour, gas; then (16C) fog, mist, depression, stupor

sky (13C from Old Norse) a cloud

aloof (nautical 16C) windward

FEELIMAGEERIES

Paraphernalia

None are so great enemies to knowledge
as they that know nothing at all

(1586)

The English language has a name for pretty much everything, even things you've never imagined needing to describe:

feazings (1825) the frayed and unravelled ends of a rope
ouch (Tudor–Stuart) the socket of a precious stone
swarf (1566) the metallic dust that accumulates after sharpening or grinding metal
ferrule (Dickens: *Nicholas Nickleby* 1838) the metal tip on an umbrella
nittiness (1664) the condition of being full of small air bubbles

DRIBS AND DRABS

If that wasn't enough, dialect supplies a few more:

charmings (Lincolnshire) paper or rag chewed into small pieces by mice
swailing (Rutland) wax drips from a candle
smut (Dublin) the remains of a nearly burnt-out candle
catamaran (Devon 1836) anything very rickety and unsafe
swiggle (East Anglia) to shake liquid in an enclosed vessel
noraleg (Shetland Isles 1899) a needle with a broken eye

ROUGHLY SPEAKING

When it comes to describing other aspects of objects, there are some surprisingly useful words out there:

scrawmax (Lincolnshire) anything badly formed or out of shape
ullage (1297) the amount of liquid by which a container falls short of being full
wee-wow (Shropshire) more on one side than on the other, ill-balanced, shaky
cattywampus (US Middle and Southern slang) diagonally across from something else
by scowl of brow (Gloucestershire) judging by the eye instead of by measurement
ostrobogulous (1951) unusual, bizarre, interesting

. . . as there are for directions too:

widdershins (1513) in the opposite direction, the wrong way
deasil (1771) clockwise, or 'in the direction of the sun's course' (considered by some to bring bad luck)
antisyzgy (1863) a union of opposites

Tahn
Dovera
Yan
Bumfit
Jiggot

COUNTING SHEEP

Being able to count was a matter of survival long before education for all. **Yan Tan Tethera** is a numerical sequence once used widely by shepherds in northern England and southern Scotland to count their sheep. It was also used in knitting to count stitches. The words differ according to accent and locale (in the Lake District versions alter according to which valley you find yourself in). In Westmorland it goes like this:

Yan · Tahn · Teddera · Meddera · Pimp (5) · Settera · Lettera · Hovera · Dovera · Dick (10) · Yan Dick · Tahn Dick · Teddera Dick · Meddera Dick · Bumfit (15) · Yan-a-Bumfit · Tahn-a Bumfit · Teddera-Bumfit · Meddera-Bumfit · Jiggot (20)

The monotonous nature of the rhyme, which would have been repeated many times during the day, also supposedly gave rise to the idea of 'counting sheep' in order to get off to sleep.

WHO WANTS TO BE A VIGINTILLIONAIRE?

When numbers give way to mathematics, things start to get a bit more daunting:

zenzizenzizenzic (1557) the eighth power of a number
lemniscate (1781) the ∞ or 'infinity' symbol
preantepenult (1791) the fourth last
shake a unit of time equal to a hundred-millionth of a second (from top secret operations during the Second World War based on the expression 'two shakes of a lamb's tail', indicating a very short time interval)
vigintillion (1857) the number expressed as a one followed by sixty-three zeros

EVEN STEVENS

Colloquial English takes delight in rhyming expressions, officially known as Reduplicative Rhyming Compounds:

nibby-gibby (Cornwall 1854) touch and go
winky-pinky (Yorkshire) a nursery word for sleepy
hockerty-cockerty (Scotland 1742) with one leg on each shoulder
inchy-pinchy (Warwickshire) the boy's game of progressive leapfrog
fidge-fadge (Yorkshire) a motion between walking and trotting
boris-noris (Dorset) careless, reckless, happy-go-lucky
wiffle-waffle (Northamptonshire) to whet one's scythes together

Shropshire, in particular, has some fine examples:

aunty-praunty (Ellesmere) high-spirited, proud
bang-swang (Clee Hills) without thought, headlong
holus-bolus impulsively, without deliberation
opple-scopple (Clun) to scramble for sweets as children do

This is a phenomenon, as these transatlantic modern versions demonstrate:

stitch 'n' bitch sewing or knitting while exchanging malicious gossip
denture venturer a long trip away from work pre-retirement
chop shop a stolen car disassembly place
zero-hero the designated driver: someone who doesn't drink alcohol at a social gathering etc. to drive those who do drink home safely

YOUR NUMBER'S UP

In the drugstores of 1930s America, staff often found it easier to talk in numerical code about certain sensitive matters:

13 a boss is roaming
14 a special order
86 we're out of what was just ordered; to refuse to serve a customer
87½ a pretty woman just walked in
95 a customer is walking out without paying
98 the manager is here

MMMMM . . .

We all know there are twenty-six letters in the alphabet. But don't think that's the end of it:

izzard (Swift 1738) an archaic name for Z
lambdoidal (1653) shaped like the letter L
tittle (1538) the little dot above the letter i (it's also the name for a pip on dice)
hyoid (1811) having a U shape
octothorpe (US 1960s) the official name of the '#' (aka the hash mark)
annodated (b.1913) anything bent somewhat like the letter S (from heraldry)
mytacism (b.1913) the incorrect or excessive use of the letter M

NEVER ODD OR EVEN: PALINDROMES

The English word palindrome was coined by the playwright Ben Jonson in around 1629 to describe words that read the same forwards as backwards; an ongoing source of fun with phrases too:

no, it is opposition
Niagara, o roar again!
rats live on no evil star
nurse, I spy gypsies, run!
murder for a jar of red rum
harass sensuousness, Sarah
a man, a plan, a canal, Panama
sums are not set as a test on Erasmus
sir, I demand - I am a maid named Iris
a new order began, a more Roman age bred Rowena

SOUND EFFECTS

Noises sometimes seem to defy description. But not in this language:

fremescence (Thomas Carlyle 1837) an incipient roaring
rimbombo (1873) a booming roar
cloop (1848) drawing a cork from a bottle
amphoric (1839) the hollow sound produced by blowing across the mouth of a bottle
wheep (Kipling: *Life's Hand* 1891) a steel weapon when drawn from a sheath
callithumpian (1836) a big parade, usually accompanied by a band of discordant instruments
rip-rap (1894 fireworks detonating)
swabble (1848) water being sloshed around
crepitation (1656) the crackling and popping sound of a wood fire
jarg (1513) the creaking of a door or gate
juck-cum-peng (Jamaican English 1943) a wooden-legged person walking
whiffle (1972) a soft sound as of gently moving air or water

TINCTURE

We can all name the primary colours: red, yellow and blue; not to mention the secondaries: purple, green and orange; after that, it's anyone's guess:

gamboge (1634) bright yellow (from gum-resin)
fulvous (1664) tawny, yellow tinged with red
ianthine (1609) violet coloured
glaucous (1671) a pale green passing into greyish blue
nacreous (1841) a pearly lustre
lyard (Chaucer *c.*1386) silvery grey almost white

VERY FLAT, NORFOLK

Dialects have their own words for colour, often reflecting the landscapes they come from:

blake (Cumberland) a yellowish golden colour
bazzom (Newfoundland) purplish tint, heather-coloured; of flesh, blue or discoloured
watchet (Midlands 1891) light blue
dunduckytimur (Norfolk and Suffolk) a dull, indescribable colour

UP BETIMES

Time waits for no man. So we might as well be certain precisely what we mean:

ughten (971) the dusk just before dawn
blue o'clock in the morning (1886) pre-dawn, when black sky gives way to purple
beetle-belch (RAF jargon) an ungodly hour
sparrow-fart (b.1910) daybreak, very early morning
beever (Sussex) eleven o'clock luncheon
upright and downstraight (Sussex) bedtime when the clock says six
blind-man's-holiday (Shropshire) twilight
cockshut (1594) evening time

PROVIDENTIAL

If you want something to come off well, choose your date with care:

Egyptian day (Yorkshire) an unlucky day, a Friday, which was a day of abstinence

pully-lug day (Cumberland 1886) a day on which traditionally ears might be pulled with impunity

cucumber time (b.1810) the quiet season in the tailoring trade (hence the expression **tailors are vegetarians** as they live on cucumber when without work)

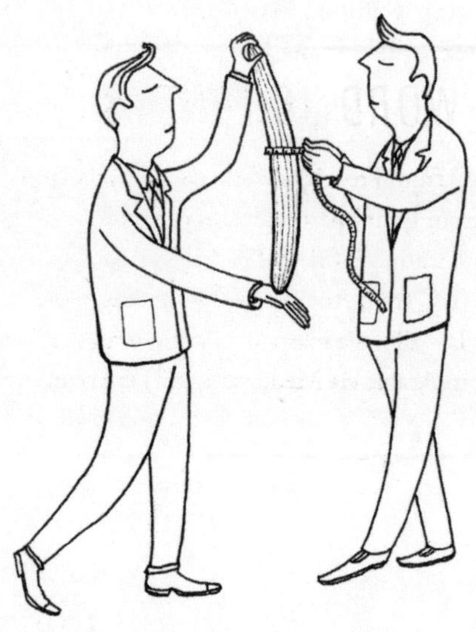

Saint Tibb's Eve (Cornwall) a day that never comes

when hens make holy water (1631) never

THINGUMMY

When all is said and done, however, there are just some things that remain very hard to put your finger on:

oojiboo (1918) an unnamed thing, a whatsit
feelimageeries (Scotland 1894) knick-knacks, odds and ends
hab nab (1580) at random, at the mercy of chance, hit or miss
gazodjule (Australian slang) a name for an object of which one cannot remember the name
floccinaucinihilipilification (1741) the categorizing of something that is useless or trivial

WORD JOURNEYS

point-blank (16C from French) a white spot (as in a target)
punctual (14C from Latin) pertinent to a point or dot
normal (17C from Latin via French) rectangular, perpendicular
paraphernalia (17C from Ancient Greek) articles of personal property which the law allows a married woman to regard as her own
algebra (14C from Arabic via Medieval Latin) the reunion of broken parts